To the Courage to
Create Brave Spaces
together!!

Warmly,

[signature]

"When the creators of Rabbinic Judaism conceived of a synagogue and its ideal leader, they had in mind Matt Gewirtz. A man of compassion and learning, probing thoughtfulness and commensurate wisdom and remarkable leadership in all seasons, Rabbi Gewirtz is beloved and revered by seemingly all in his community. In this remarkable memoir/reflection, readers everywhere can do what his congregants have for a quarter century—learn from and grow with a master."

–**Mark Gerson, Chairman of United Hatzalah and Author of** *The Telling: How Judaism's Essential Book Reveals the Meaning of Life*

"Clergy have a front row to the most intense moments of people's lives, like marriage and birth, death and divorce. And yet there are very few excellent memoirs by clergy (maybe it's because they spend so much time writing sermons). So it's especially auspicious to get this touching, thoughtful book, in which a leading rabbi candidly discusses his own journey, from his own childhood as an indifferent student through his years as a spiritual first responder to 9/11, COVID, and more."

–**Mark Oppenheimer, author of** *Squirrel Hill: The Tree of Life Synagogue Shooting and the Soul of a Neighborhood*

TO BUILD

—A—

BRAVE SPACE

The MAKING *of a* SPIRITUAL
FIRST RESPONDER

TO BUILD

— A —

BRAVE SPACE

The MAKING *of a* SPIRITUAL
FIRST RESPONDER

Rabbi Matthew D. Gewirtz

POST HILL PRESS

A POST HILL PRESS BOOK
ISBN: 978-1-64293-542-4
ISBN (eBook): 978-1-64293-543-1

To Build a Brave Space:
The Making of a Spiritual First Responder
© 2022 by Rabbi Matthew D. Gewirtz
All Rights Reserved

Cover design by Tiffani Shea

This is a work of nonfiction. All people, locations, events, and situation are portrayed to the best of the author's memory.

Post Hill Press
New York • Nashville
posthillpress.com

Published in the United States of America
1 2 3 4 5 6 7 8 9 10

You left but have never stopped imparting your wisdom. Without your unique brand of love and devotion, I would not be me.

To my loving Parents: Tabitha D. Gewirtz and Arthur D. Gewirtz. Pop, my mind comes from you. Mom, my heart, and soul come from you.

To two of my most significant mentors of life:

Rabbi Alan Abraham Kay, your soulful, deep, and light-filled smile, guide my path daily.

Rabbi Aaron D. Panken, your intelligence, determination, and humor are of those qualities I will never let go. Your untimely passing in one I will never reconcile.

I devote this work to you to help manifest the lessons you planted within me.

CONTENTS

PREFACE

I'd served over ten years as the rabbi of Congregation B'nai Jeshurun in Short Hills, New Jersey, when I found myself protesting at Newark Airport in January of 2017. As the son of left-leaning activists, marching for causes was nothing new to me. Our parents raised us to participate in peaceful protest and to use our voices in times of injustice. So when my wife and I heard that a crowd was gathering at the airport to protest what would be the first of many controversial moves our then-president would make—banning people from certain Muslim countries from entering the United States—we didn't hesitate to head straight there, kids in tow. At the time, it was widely and mistakenly believed that the ban was based on ethnicity alone rather than on the countries in question being on a watch list. But the news media was in a frenzy, and my family and I got caught up in the whirlwind.

When we arrived, the atmosphere was tense. A few hundred people were already gathered, expressing their fears over this new presidency based on its early actions. Soon, there were thousands of people, including local politicians and media, in the crowd. My family and I circled with the others, holding makeshift signs with slogans like "We too were foreigners," until we began to hear anti-Israel chants rising. At this point, my kids were both nervous and confused, and my wife and I felt that familiar, sinking sensation that rises up with expressions of blatant anti-Semitism. That was when we left.

Still in shock over the election results and on high alert, I wrote my congregants a letter to explain why I felt the need to take a public stand and cross the partisan line I generally avoided in my professional role as a rabbi. I encouraged them to join me in upholding our shared values and fighting for what we, as a community, surely believed.

Our Jewish history, I reminded them, was one of incessant migration. We were slaves in Egypt. We were victims of persecution during the crusades, inquisitions, and the Holocaust. We wandered from country to country looking for acceptance and religious freedom. We have been hungry and homeless time and again. And although we have found acceptance, nourishment, and places to belong, we are taught to remember the experiences of our ancestors. Every year at Passover we are instructed to tell the story of our enslavement and liberation so that each generation can understand that experience as if it was their own. We implore our communities to welcome immigrants, for we too were once strangers in a strange land.

The idea of banning Muslims or any other group based on their ethnicity alone, or by association with a few acknowledged "bad apples," was a visceral affront to Jewish values. It seemed reasonable to expect that whether or not they would choose to stand with me in opposition to the policy at the airport, the majority of my congregation would agree with my decision to do so.

Such was not the case.

Almost immediately after publishing my letter, all hell broke loose. Two families left the congregation that very day, and others threatened to follow suit. I was characterized as a "rabbi who only cared about money, brainwashed children, and didn't care about those who voted on the right," by an anonymous group of congregants. These members argued that I was guilty of conflating Judaism with Democratic politics and that I was using my pulpit and my classrooms to spread my own version of liberal values under the guise of Jewish practice.

After a decade with my congregation, I understood that our large membership of nearly five thousand people was hardly monolithic, and that there were many in our midst who had voted for and supported Donald Trump. But I couldn't have imagined that my one act of protest would result in over thirty hours of phone calls and hundreds of emails.

What I saw unfolding was a microcosm of the country at large at that time—and for at least the next four years. Our sense of community was at risk as each side dug in and refused to listen to the other. Frustration and anger were the go-to emotions in those days. It seemed impossible to find middle ground.

Weeks earlier, after Trump's inauguration, I'd written a prayer for the health and spirit of the new president, conveying my hopes for a peaceful and prosperous term despite my own political opposition. Part of my calling as a spiritual leader is to set an example of acceptance, tolerance, and good will, especially in trying times.

When that earlier letter was published, I heard from everyone. From those on the left, I was excoriated for simply acknowledging Trump as the president. Doing so apparently linked me to misogyny, sexism, and racism. From the right, I was accused of being pedantically apologetic, as if by praying for him I was saying that he was so ill-equipped to hold office, he needed my help. An act meant to open minds was met with hardened hearts.

The same thing happened when my participation in the airport protest became public. My social media exploded with threats and insults from the general public. And in my own congregation, almost every interaction I had that week began with anger.

Still, I managed to start each conversation, as I always do, by asking about the welfare of the caller's family. This simple gesture of human concern—which we pastoral leaders use to lower the temperature of a conflict almost immediately—works every time, simply because when you ask after someone's loved ones, their usual response is to soften and ask about yours in return. In this way, we remind ourselves that beneath the fervent emotions of the moment, we are all just people, with lives and children, jobs and dreams, and we allow ourselves to truly listen to what the other person has to say.

Presidents of congregational communities have unique and special relationships with their clergy. They play the paradoxical role of both sacred partner and supervisor. If forged effectively, the relationship is one of symbiotic partnership; the hierarchical nature of the connection is utilized only when necessary. Otherwise, the dialogue is free-flowing and replete with wise counsel.

In this case, the president of my synagogue, though publicly supportive of my decision, privately wondered if it was a good use of my time to spend so many hours on the phone fielding questions about this act of protest, especially since so many callers just seemed to want to vent their displeasure with me. I explained that I thought this was my job. And as the week progressed, I heard stories that deepened my connection to these people who I consider my community.

One congregant told me about his father, who had been killed by Islamic terrorists long before 9/11, when such a thing was not part of our collective awareness. To him, as a teenager, the circumstances were as unfathomable as they were tragic. He didn't know if he could ever trust Muslims again, and he was still filled with anger and hate as a result. From his perspective, we needed to be more vigilant, both in our country at large and as Jews in particular, and more aware of the threats of Muslim terrorism. For him, Trump's travel ban seemed justified and understandable. He found value in being proactive about preventing possible terrorists from entering the country, ensuring that other families would not suffer a similar loss.

Another member had immigrated to the United States as a child. He and his family were forced to spend six months in a holding center in Europe while they were thoroughly vetted. He told me that every minute of those months was worthwhile because becoming a citizen in the United States was the privilege of his lifetime. He believed strongly that American-born citizens, unaware of the realities of living under an autocratic regime, take their rights for granted. If we are not vigilant enough in protecting our country, he thought, we risk devolving into the kind of society he had fled.

Others questioned my motivations for getting involved in the protest: Was this about religion or politics? Was our Temple merely an extension of the Democratic Party? If so, how would members of other parties fit in? The immigrant member wondered aloud if his family would be stripped of their rights to believe differently if they remained. He had waited a long time to be able to practice Judaism freely; now he was beginning to feel confined in a new and unfamiliar way.

Some of these conversations were about why we experience hate and feel bias and about how we can raise children in a world in which we fear and distrust others. We talked about the ability to both vet potential threats and show compassion. We agreed there were many paths forward to our common goals and that we all wanted to live in a country of safety and openness. These talks rarely concluded with agreement, but they all ended with increased respect and understanding, opening the possibility for repair even if none of us yet knew that healing was needed. It was a chance for us to prove we could break from the national path of impending polarization.

By the end of that week, I realized that although we were headed for a tumultuous time in America, we had an opportunity within our own spiritual community to engage one another and participate in difficult conversations. There was much conflict ahead but perhaps just as much potential. Our synagogue could be a shining example of living and thriving together even as our worldviews grew more disparate by the day.

I wrote to the membership to thank them for the gift of dialogue, for the opportunity to grow as a community, and to invite them to Friday night services at which I planned to speak about lessons in religious Jewish and societal discourse. On an average Friday night, three hundred people show up for services. That night, we had over five hundred.

* * *

Little did I know how much worse things were about to get in this country and how many obstacles we would face as a community and as a nation. Beyond the tremendous political upheaval of the Trump presidency and the division and disillusionment that came to the surface as a result, we saw outrage over racial injustice after the killing of George Floyd, a barrage of gun violence nationwide, devastating environmental crises, an epidemic of depression and isolation in our age of social media, and a deadly global pandemic. At times it felt as though the world might literally fall apart.

The social order we'd taken for granted was unraveling globally. Closer to home, my synagogue felt the effects of these years in numerous ways, and it was my job to stay on top of things and help my congregants find meaning, purpose, and even joy in troubling times, as rabbis throughout history had done. So many nights I'd lay awake wondering how we got here and how we'd get through. What did it all mean for us, and how could I present a vision of hope and healing that was genuine and grounded in reality as well as in Jewish tradition?

My congregation is one bubble, one world unto itself, in the vast Venn diagram of American life, overlapping with so many other bubbles. It's my job to counsel and comfort and experience life alongside my congregants, and doing so has been and continues to be the great privilege of my lifetime. Being a rabbi has offered me a glimpse into many versions of the same reality and given me the chance to break out of my own comfort zone, to see the world through different lenses, and to grow personally through my professional experiences.

When you answer the call of becoming a cleric, no matter which faith tradition you follow, you agree to look people in the eye and do your best to come up with plausible answers when they ask supremely existential questions: What is the purpose of life? Why do bad things happen to good people? Why are people so nasty to one another? Is there life after death? Is there really a Messiah? Do Jews believe in Heaven and Hell? If so, how do I get to one and avoid the other? Can you pray for good weather for my child's wedding? Why should I care for others when they don't seem to care for me? I don't always like my children or spouse, and I am not sure they always like me, so how can we make it as a family? I hate my job, but it pays me a bundle…what should I do? Is there a God? Does God hear me when I talk to Him (or Her)? The list goes on.

I was trained to engage with these matters of the heart on a daily basis, and I do my best to do so with compassion and patience. But no amount of training could have prepared me for those years when so much in the world around us shifted, seemingly all at once.

I believe the best way to infuse your life with deeper meaning and purpose in the here and now is to reflect on where you come from and where you hope to go. Some people may assume that rabbis sit around all day pondering life's great questions in a constant state of meditation, hoping to reach a great spiritual awakening. The truth is that being a rabbi of a large congregation is much like being the CEO of a business. It's busy. There are life cycle events to manage, holidays to celebrate, and sermons to write, but there are also board meetings to attend, budgets to balance, and community outreach to organize. As a pastoral leader, I often struggle to find the "work/spirit" balance. A day in the life of a rabbi, as with so many other professions, can be simultaneously draining and exhilarating. But after nearly twenty-five years of doing this, I find that, while the business end of things fills much of my time, it's the spiritual work I do with my congregants that gives me the greatest sense of accomplishment.

Writing this book has been an exercise in reflection and growth. I began the process by expressing my own political vision and my hopes for the future during a trying time in American history. Then the Coronavirus pandemic swept the world, and my focus shifted to documenting the experience of shepherding a large congregation through a uniquely difficult and spiritually charged time.

Life became intensely complicated and difficult for all of us. The question of how to pastor to people who were isolated from one another was a real challenge. The idea of an elongated crisis was also a serious struggle. No one knew what to expect and how long to expect it. The unknown lurked at every turn, not to mention the ravaging impact of the virus itself. As the statistics would bear out, we had scores of people who contracted the Coronavirus, and too many died—and died quickly. Beyond bringing comfort to those who were physically sick, we had to do anything we could to help people cope with their sense of isolation. We livestreamed, Zoomed, Facetimed, Skyped—anything to help people feel they were not alone. Additionally, I wrote a bi-weekly letter to the congregation with ideas about how to make meaning and purpose out of a time that seemed meaningless.

At first, people were just plain scared. Next came anxiety, followed by depression and resentment. Before long, so much collective tension had built up that it seemed anything could blow at any time. Of course, the pandemic raged at the same time that the country was already dangerously polarized in terms of politics and policy, and that combination proved to be toxic. For many of us, the tipping point came after we watched the videotape of George Floyd being killed in broad daylight by a police officer. Anger over racial injustice broke forth as many Americans wondered how much more we could take. As protests and rallies took place all over the country, we clergy had to strike a balance between supporting, comforting, and protecting the community, which was still at risk of an airborne contagion on top of everything else. Our main source of communication remained the Internet, a problematic and biased space to begin with.

And once we began to see the end of that horrific historical moment and started our slow and steady journey to a "new normal," my sense of transformation and revelation took hold, and the focus of my writing shifted yet again.

We are all telling our own stories, living our own truths day to day. Those stories change and evolve as we take each of life's unexpected turns. In the end, I decided to tell my own story of what it means to me to serve a community, why I chose to live a life of service and faith, and how my expression of that service has changed and evolved over many years and finally led me to a vision for the future that I hope to work to embody as I move forward in my rabbinate.

My story, like so many of yours, is one of learning to accept new realities and shifting perspective with time and experience. I'm grateful to be able to share it with you in these pages.

CHAPTER ONE:

They're All Gone

B y the time the terrible news broke, I ought to have been in bed. It was September 5, 1972, my first day of second grade, and getting late for a school night—9:24 p.m., to be exact. I wasn't tired, but even so, sleep was impossible. The world I knew had suddenly begun to wobble on its axis.

The kitchen radio had been tuned all day to my parents' favorite station, 1010 WINS—"All news, all the time." The same sort of broadcast chatter could be heard through the open windows and across the front lawns of homes up and down our block in Lynbrook, Long Island, a middle-class neighborhood of stolid, single-family homes a few blocks from the Queens border.

In the living room, my dad, an English professor at nearby Hofstra University, was sitting on the edge of the sofa, staring transfixed at the television. My mom, a teacher, stood motionless in the doorway to the dining room, one eye on her kids, the other towards the TV.

On the screen, a man in a pale-yellow jacket was talking to the camera. At the bottom was a digital display: *3:24 a.m. Munich Time.*

"This is Jim McKay, speaking to you live from ABC headquarters just outside the Olympic village in Munich, West Germany. Our worst fears have been realized tonight. They've now said that there were eleven hostages. Two were killed in their rooms yesterday morning. Nine were killed at the airport tonight." He shook his head. "They're all gone." "They" were Jews.

A team of armed Palestinian terrorists calling themselves Black September had invaded a dormitory at the XX Olympic Games in Munich. They took eleven hostages—Israeli athletes and their coaches—and, in exchange for their lives, demanded the release of more than two hundred Palestinians imprisoned in Israel.

Israel's fourth prime minister, Golda Meir (dubbed the Iron Lady), had refused to negotiate. For most of the day it seemed the crisis would somehow resolve itself. It was unthinkable that anyone could be so callous as to actually execute innocent young athletes and coaches. But a fumbled attempt by the German police to set a trap for the hostage-takers erupted into a shootout. The terrorists turned their weapons on the hostages, whose hands and feet were bound, and slaughtered them without mercy.

The Munich Massacre, as it came to be known, was an inflection point in modern history—one of those 9/11 moments when the rotation of the Earth seems to pause, and you sense nothing will ever be quite the same. It was a terrible picture never imagined, forever imprinted in my mind. From then on, not only did I understand that terrorism was a part of our social fabric, I also knew that there was always a possibility of my being killed for no reason other than my Jewish identity. I didn't even have to be religious—it wouldn't matter to the terrorists.

The realization was mind-boggling for a young child, but not particularly surprising. I was a seven-year-old Jewish boy. No one had to sit me down and teach me the principal narrative of Jewish history. For Jews of my generation, it was impossible to grow up in New York without knowing people who were Holocaust survivors, or who had lost relatives in the war, or who simply hated everything German just by association. Although the Holocaust itself was an infrequent topic of conversation, the institutional and social anti-Semitism of thousands of years of Jewish history always lurked just beneath the surface.

I heard the stories of Jewish struggles and survival in synagogue during the Holy Days. The details I picked up at the dinner table. I was an ardent eavesdropper on adults, hanging on every word when they spoke about relatives who were lost in the Holocaust. Half of my father's family perished in those years—his paternal grandparents, aunts and uncles, and at least two dozen cousins. The loss was unfathomable. I still vividly remember my father telling me of his grandmother's violent death. His relatives reported that her head had been cut off and then sent rolling down the gutter. I would ask him over and over again about the story, because I couldn't believe something so barbaric was actually possible. Even now, I am struck by the matter-of-fact manner in which my father told me the story (which, I imagine, was the same way it was told to him). That was the way of his generation—rather than ponder the difficult realities of their lives, they focused on moving forward.

My father's Uncle Chaim was one of those presumed lost until one day, a couple years after the war, he showed up on my grandmother's Brooklyn doorstep. He'd been in Poland and then sent to prison in Russia. She hadn't seen him in fourteen years, since he was eight years old. I wasn't there to experience their reunion first-hand, of course, but I can still remember how vividly my father described that day. His mother fainted when she saw him— the baby brother she believed had died years before—the emotion of his miraculous return overwhelming her. The story was one that loomed large in our family's oral history, and my siblings and I never tired of hearing the tale of the missing brother's belated homecoming.

Like many survivors, Uncle Chaim didn't talk about his experiences in the camps. We wanted details, and we had so many questions for him. But back then, survivors instinctively kept their stories to themselves. Not only were their memories painful and difficult to share, but they also struggled with the public perception that they must have been weak for "allowing" themselves to be taken prisoner. Until the capture and trial of Adolph Eichmann, architect of the extermination program, the world didn't realize just how methodically the Nazis lulled six million Jews and four million other "enemies of the state" into submission until it was too late to fight back.

I vividly remember tugging on my father's arm in a jewelry store, intensely curious to know why the salesman had a number tattooed on his arm. He shushed me with a stern look. Later, he explained about the systemic way Hitler and his complicit followers methodically killed six million of our ancestors. He wasn't admonishing, but solemnly hinting that we Jews couldn't trust anyone. He lived with the fear that this could happen again when we least expected it.

Although my father didn't appear to be living in fear for his safety, when tragedies like the Munich Massacres happened, when Jews or Israelis were targeted, something snapped him back to this primal instinct. He lived with the knowledge that there would always be plenty of people who hated Jews, and therefore we should always be on guard. Growing up knowing that half of his family was murdered for no reason other than their faith legitimated that ever-present fear for him.

As a young adult, I had a hard time reconciling my father's professional life with his personal biases. He was a professor of Shakespearian literature. He lived to open the minds of his students to every perspective possible. He believed that fine academic training was integral to the inner development of his students and their trajectories in life. How could someone so open to the depths of understanding be so insistent that the whole world was anti-Semitic? But as I myself matured, both intellectually and spiritually, I understood that his childhood experience had locked him into a mentality from which it was impossible to break free. Unfortunately, the world didn't give him many reasons to think differently.

My mother's family, on the other hand, had arrived in America before World War II, her grandfather having emigrated from Russia at age fourteen to flee the pogroms. Though they were lucky enough to have evaded the Holocaust, generations of persecution and anti-Semitism created a family who were vocal socialists, civil rights activists, anti-Vietnam War protesters, and confirmed atheists. None of them (much like my father's side of the family) would even think of buying so much as a toothpick made in Germany, let alone a Volkswagen.

But even though my mother was ardently opposed to war and would have done anything to discourage me from joining the American army to fight in a war like Vietnam, she was a committed Zionist and would have been proud to see me fight for Israel. This was the kind of cognitive dissonance that I accepted as normal as a child. Israel would always be the exception to our philosophical rule of thumb, and our Judaism would always trump our nationalism as Americans.

That night in 1972, I experienced a new, visceral awareness of my Jewishness and began my own lifelong devotion to the Jewish homeland. The Munich Massacre was a vivid moment in the history of our tribe, and it was being written in blood right before the eyes of millions around the world. In the intensely personal way that children perceive big events, it immediately became imprinted on me as my history as well.

There had been terrorist attacks before, but this was the incident that woke Israel and the rest of the world to the potential for ever more devastating attacks on non-combatants, and the possibility of numerous civilian casualties. In one of those improbable-but-true coincidences, while Israeli Olympians were being murdered in Munich in September 1972, workmen were putting the final touches on the World Trade Center Twin Towers. Twenty-nine years later, Islamic terrorists would destroy those buildings, killing nearly three-thousand people and changing the course of our history yet again.

The Olympics attack was pure, twisted genius—timed during an event that would be watched live by people everywhere, a grim television first. For the first time since 1936, Germany (West Germany, at the time) was hosting the Games. For its slogan, host officials chose *Die Heiteren Spiele*—"The Cheerful Games." The Germans were eager to demonstrate to the world that life and society had changed there, decades after the brutality. To that end, their security guards wore street clothes to blend in—powder blue leisure suits with white golf caps—and carried no visible weapons.

For my family, Israel's participation in the 1972 Olympic Games was personal, a moment of tribal pride with the potential for a bit of symbolic payback. Wouldn't it be great if Jews beat the Germans in wrestling? Imagine that!

My parents had explained to my siblings and me that just five years earlier, Israel's survival as a nation seemed to have passed a crucial test during a war with Egypt—the Six-Day War of 1967. The conflict was ostensibly over Egypt's attempt to blockade one of Israel's vital waterways. But that was just the trigger. Egypt, Syria, and Jordan were out to destroy the Jewish state of Israel. Instead, Israel came out of the conflict having seized the Gaza Strip and the entire Sinai Peninsula up to the Nile River from Egypt; from Jordan, the West Bank, including the holy epicenter (for Jews, Muslims, and Christians) of East Jerusalem; and from Syria, the militarily vital Golan Heights. The armed forces of all of Israel's three principal enemies had been shredded and no longer posed the threat that it had in previous decades. For us, as kids, that story was awe-inspiring, on the level of the greatest superhero narratives. The Israeli army loomed large in our imaginations as impossibly strong, able to overcome the greatest odds.

By the time of the 1972 Olympic Games, Jews around the world were feeling hopeful about Israel's future. The country had become so strong that its enemies could never defeat it, so of course they wouldn't think of trying. The symbolism of Jews being welcomed in Germany and participating in an event as serene, egalitarian, and wholesome as the Olympics was evidence that the Jewish homeland was durable and real peace was possible.

Then came the brutality of the Munich murders, made even more shocking by the fact that they happened on German soil while under the protection of West German authorities. It was inexcusable. Security had been so lax that the terrorists—who disguised themselves as athletes with gym bags full of weapons— were able to get a boost over the fence and into the compound from some Canadian athletes who had been out partying and thought they were being helpful. I can remember learning the details of this attack and going over and over them in my mind, as though they were scenes in a movie. I wanted to know how the "good guys" would seek revenge and how it would all end for Israel.

That week, we went to Friday night Shabbat services at our Reform synagogue, Temple Emanu-El. All across the country and around the world, Jews were doing the same, expressing their grief, reaffirming their heritage, and demonstrating their solidarity.

On that day I found a lifetime role model in our rabbi, Harold Saperstein. At services, Rabbi Saperstein announced that he was going to fast for eleven days—one day for every Israeli who had been murdered in Munich. He invited the congregation to do the same. This fascinated me. I only knew about fasting in the context of Yom Kippur, and I was too young to have started doing it myself. For a seven-year-old, the idea of even one day without food was inconceivable. On the way home, I asked my father if Rabbi Saperstein was really going to go eleven days without eating. "How can he do that? Won't he die?"

"He's going to fast during the day and only eat at night," my father explained.

"Why is he doing that?"

"Because that's what we do," he said. "Fasting is a way of showing that we stand up for each other, to express grief, and to show that each of our lives matter."

I was too young to grasp it intellectually, but on some level I understood the symbolism of giving something up, the spiritual imperative of ritual. To me, this seemed to be the most selfless expression of solidarity and mourning—an action far beyond my own capabilities but one I understood. I understood it all the more because my rabbi combined the things I cared about most as a kid—sports, food, and Judaism—to make a stand with the clarity of superlative morality. I didn't understand it all, but it indelibly seared my young spirit.

As I grew up and came to know more about Rabbi Saperstein, the deeper my admiration for him became. He had been a chaplain in Europe during World War II. He had worked to recover the history of the Jewish community in the German city of Worms. He fought for the rights of Soviet Jewry and spoke publicly of their plight as early as 1959. As an influential force in the Reform Judaism movement, his focus was more on action than ritual. He was a committed Zionist who had visited Israel many times, most notably during the Six-Day War in 1967. As a result, he was one of the first Jews in two decades to be able to visit Jerusalem's Old City and to pray at the Western Wall when it was liberated. He lived history, which made him something of a Jewish rock star in my eyes.

My family was not the most observant in the neighborhood, but we were committed to our synagogue, and my father insisted we have Shabbat dinner every Friday night. After a few preliminary, but not perfunctory blessings and exchanges of hugs, we inevitably broke into a rambunctious, passionate, loud political conversation that most of the time was a lot of fun. These discussions taught my siblings and me the imperative of making our world better using civics and action as paths to make our country and our world a kinder and more generous.

At those dinners, we learned so much about our parents and grandparents, their values and their interests. My mother proudly and defiantly described herself sneaking out of her parents' house for days at a time to march in the South for civil rights. Anti-Vietnam posters were plastered on our walls, and I remember many nights when my home was filled with organizers working to elect any candidate who promised to bring the war to an end. My mother was a Red Diaper Baby. I never understood why my Great Aunt Sadie could never visit us in New York until it was explained that she had been forced to run away to Los Angeles because she was a self-declared communist.

Needless to say, I was raised to abhor injustice and to fight with both my words and actions to do my part in balancing the scales of justice for anyone who was not whole. My siblings and I were taught to fight against bigotry, hatred, prejudice, and inequality. I didn't know it then, but my entire upbringing was intrinsically linked to our Jewish life. Everything, from the left-wing ways of my mother's family, which were enmeshed in the world of Yiddish culture and the *Shula* education system (the Yiddish cultural, secular equivalent of a synagogue religious school), to the passionate political conversations that took place around our Shabbat dinner table, was based on the idea that Jews were meant, by way of our faith, to do our part in fixing the world.

Though never told so explicitly, I was taught implicitly that to be a good Jew was also to be a Democrat. We voted against our pocketbooks, choosing to pay more in taxes for the causes we championed because our ethics were more important than our bank accounts. Our values made us stand up for those who were downtrodden. I am grateful to have grown up with such strong fiber, but in hindsight, I realize that I was raised without being taught how to recognize the difference between my religion and my politics. At home, they seemed to go hand in hand. Being aligned with the Democratic party appeared to be the clearest path to justice, and only much later in life as I grew in my career as a rabbi, would I come to question that assumption.

Rabbi Saperstein inculcated the same caliber of values. He stood no taller than five-foot-six, but he spoke with a backbone that moved me, even as a young child, to want to make the world better. Even now, I can see him pushing and prodding us, his congregation, to bring about positive change, simply because it was the Jewish thing to do.

That night after the Munich Massacre, we sat in our synagogue in silence. No one could make sense of how this had happened. How could it have occurred in Germany, of all places,

where Jewish blood had so recently covered the ground in expo-
nential amounts? If this could happen at the Olympics, it could
happen anywhere. We were dismayed, frightened, and a bit lost.
How would this blatant anti-Semitism filter down to our families
in New York? Would we face animosity at public school or in our
neighborhood parks? At synagogue, we hoped to find solace in
prayer and in one another, and to find a way to make sense of the
senseless.

I wish I remembered the exact words of Rabbi Saperstein's
sermon, because I think in large part, that sermon is responsible
for inspiring me to become a rabbi myself. When he announced
that he would fast for eleven days in memory of the eleven lost
souls, he essentially created a unique mourning ritual for his
community. By fasting himself and offering his congregants the
option of adopting this new practice, he allowed us to join hands
and express our collective grief, our profound sadness. From
there, we could pray from the bottom of our hearts and then
stand up against hatred and bigotry and never hide our pride for
the unique nature of our community, faith, and history.

Rabbi Saperstein gave us something tactile in the face of our
amorphous disorientation, making us realize we had a responsibility to take part in making an unjust world better. He charis-
matically implored us to stand up for what we believe in. He fed
our souls with the belief that our hands would find the power
to act. As a young boy I loved sports and food above all else.
Ritualizing food to mourn athletes spoke to me on a primal level.
It was something I would remember for the rest of my life. From
then on, I associated Judaism with a moral and civil code I could
use to enact change for justice in the world.

Not only did that experience around Munich in 1972 propel me to the rabbinate, it was also a moment in history that forever linked religion and politics for me. All the emotion I felt at home and at synagogue conflated the two in what I would later recognize as a sometimes unhealthy manner of thinking. I got the emotion as well as the motivation to act, but it would be years before I understood the intellectual substance that bolstered my positions.

Harold Saperstein was among the best rabbis of his generation, but he was not unique in raising us to act in accordance with the prophetic voice. Indeed, Saperstein and other sacred teachers taught us, a whole generation of rabbis and Jews, to see our faith as motivation to put the pieces of our world back together. They wanted us to manifest a messianic age in which we would feed the hungry, clothe the naked, and free the oppressed.

Throughout my childhood, it was as though a circuit was being intricately wired into my system that eventually became the essence of my being. This is the foundation upon which my adult identity was built. The stitching together of the passion for politics and religion at home was matched almost equally by my rabbi and congregation. Rabbi Saperstein and my parents' call has never left me. It was a springboard from which action and faith became equal partners in guiding my purpose forward.

* * *

One year and a month after the murder of the eleven Israeli athletes, our family attended Yom Kippur services at Temple Emanu-El. The Day of Atonement is the holiest day of the Jewish year. Traditionally marked by a day-long fast, prayer, and extended services in the synagogue, it is a self-reflective moment when Jews acknowledge and atone for their mistakes and get a fresh start for the new Jewish year. This holiday is observed in every Jewish community, and it is the one day each year when even completely secular Jews who never pray or set foot inside a synagogue will often show up for services.

Yom Kippur 1973 fell on a mild, bright fall day, October 6. The leaves had begun to turn but were still on the trees. It was an especially quiet Saturday in New York and its suburbs because the metropolitan region is home to the largest Jewish population in the world outside of Israel. Virtually all Jewish-owned businesses were closed. The synagogues were full to capacity and then some.

About eight hundred families belonged to the Emanu-El congregation, so the sanctuary on this day was full of relatives and friends exchanging greetings and catching up on life. It started out as a very typical holiday experience. But no sooner had the service started than someone interrupted Rabbi Saperstein to whisper in his ear. He turned to the congregation and spoke with great urgency.

I wasn't paying attention to what he said, but I remember the gasps. A murmur ran through the crowd, and suddenly we were all being shooed out of our seats and hurried out the door. My father led us straight to the car and drove home. It was a bizarre, unexpected experience.

In the back seat, in bewildered silence, my siblings (Liz, ten, Josh, seven, and Rachel, four) and I huddled together like baby birds. We knew something was wrong, but we had no idea what was happening. As my father gunned the engine through a yellow light, he muttered to us over his shoulder, "There's a war on in Israel."

Six time zones away, on that beautiful fall day in New York, the armed forces of Egypt, Syria, and eight other Arab nations launched a massive, surprise air and land strike that—by all accounts—came close to turning Israel into a country occupied by murderous Jew haters. On Yom Kippur in Israel, the quiet is many times what we experience in New York. The country is essentially shut down; no one works or drives, schools and businesses are closed, all but essential military personnel are home with their families, and observant Jews unplug their electrical appliances, including radios and phones. At 2 p.m. at the quietest time on the quietest day of the year, emerging from a huge cloud of dust, came thousands of tanks and thousands of artillery pieces from Egypt in the south and Syria in the north. Fighter jets soared overhead. It was a full-scale invasion.

The Munich massacre had put Jews on notice that no gathering was safe. Now, perhaps because of a bomb threat or just as a precaution, our Yom Kippur service on the other side of the world had been interrupted and everyone was sent home.

There was an unfamiliar pitch of panic in the voices of my mother and father. Articles about Munich had just been in the newspapers, reminding us of the anniversary of the attack. We had just been remembering the trauma of that event, and we were still processing it ourselves one year later. Now, something much worse was happening to the Jews of Israel—*in* Israel.

If Munich had jolted me out of my childhood innocence, the Yom Kippur War gave me horrible, vivid nightmares. The tension our family had experienced during the hostage crisis was nothing compared to the raw fear that crackled through our lives for the next week. Israel is the only place in the world where being Jewish does not mean either being tolerated or targeted, and if it was decimated on the holiest day of our religious year, how would we ever recover?

The invasion was a vivid David versus Goliath match-up and another instance of twisted genius. Israel was outgunned, outmanned, and outmaneuvered. Every day, the New York newspapers devoted page after page to stories about the war. Even though I was still such a young kid, I read them all: "Copters with Israeli Wounded Land at Hospital All Day." "Israelis Report 'Piles' of Egyptian Dead." One report said the Syrians had fired a 1,000-pound Soviet-built missile that destroyed a complex of buildings on a kibbutz, a cooperative farm, where 270 children would have been sleeping had they not been moved to a safe shelter. I pictured myself as one of those kids, awakened in the middle of the night and told to run for my life.

Among other factors, the country was saved by some very brave Israeli soldiers whose quick thinking and fearlessness held the attacking forces off just long enough for reserves to be assembled and reinforcements deployed. Many of them died doing so. The US was essential, airlifting massive amounts of military supplies.

I remember being obsessed with the historical facts surrounding the conflict and doing my best to memorize them. The Yom Kippur War was a series of epic tank battles aimed at retaking land that Israel had occupied since the 1967 Six-Day War. With Egypt, the field of battle was south, in the vast, parched, empty Sinai Peninsula. In Israel's north, the conflict was with Syria over control of the Golan Heights, a strategic ridge over-looking a wide, sparsely populated valley.

Syria threw an estimated 1,200 Russian tanks straight at the Israeli positions, which were defended by just 170 tanks. When the last shot was fired, both sides had been badly bloodied, but Syria got the worst of it and withdrew—just as the Israeli defense was about to collapse—leaving behind the smoking hulks of five hundred Soviet-made tanks. Israel had miraculously been saved.

That battle made military history and was portrayed in doz-ens of documentaries and in a wrenching 2020 Israeli television series, *Valley of Tears*. Not until many years later would the world learn that Israel was in such a dire situation that it briefly con-sidered deploying tactical nuclear weapons—or at least made such a convincing threat to do so that the attackers abandoned their efforts.

Details that emerged over time about the behavior of the Egyptian and Syrian soldiers have made clear how real the poten-tial was for a genocidal event. Some two dozen Israeli prisoners of war were found bound and shot through the head, Nazi-style. Some enemy soldiers were caught in possession of body parts they had cut off of dead Israeli soldiers for souvenirs.

For many months after the war, I would wake up at night from terrifying dreams about burning tanks and Israelis being killed. I was consumed by all of it. My parents were so over-whelmed themselves that they never thought to talk to us kids and explain what was going on or even ask us how we were doing. Eventually, the crisis would pass, and Israel would go on to develop a legendary defense force and a rich, complex society, not to mention a technology industry that is the envy of the world. But back then, all I knew was that I feared for Israel—and for Jews everywhere—as we seemed to be under attack wherever we went.

The war that nearly destroyed Israel ended up making it stronger. American Jews who moved to Israel were quoted in our local newspapers about their steadfast commitment to the Jewish state, despite the violence that seemed to always be around the corner. One of our neighbors from Lynbrook had moved to Israel and joined the IDF. To know a name and face on the front lines made it all seem so real to me, and so relatable. I understood my personal connection to this far-away land, and that connection made my imagination come to life.

After the Yom Kippur War, I recall noticing (perhaps for the first time) the way the Israeli flag was prominently displayed in our synagogue. As with most American congregations, we had an American flag on one side of the ark (where the Torah scrolls are kept) and an Israeli flag on the other. We took for granted that we American Jews had a great love for both countries. Although I had not yet been to Israel, I felt inherently connected to the country of my forefathers now that I had lived through these two major historical events. What I didn't yet realize was how important the synagogue itself would become as I carried that connection with me and ventured into adulthood.

CHAPTER TWO:

Evolving Through Paradox

When I was ten, my parents divorced. We left Long Island and thereafter divided our time between the Upper West Side of Manhattan, where my mother lived and where we went to school during the week, and Brooklyn, where we spent weekends with my dad. It was a trying experience for us kids to understand that, although we loved our parents deeply and they loved us unconditionally in return, they were fundamentally incompatible.

For the next few years, I found myself playing the role of child-arbiter, trying to keep the peace between my parents and their extended families, who barely tolerated each other. Although the negotiating skills I developed as a result would serve me well in the long run, at the time, I was just a devastated kid, reeling from the rift in my family.

During those same years, conflict seemed to find me everywhere I went. I was mugged so often that after the first dozen or so times I gave up counting. What I recall is mostly a blur of indignities: my schoolbag being dumped out on the sidewalk, and its contents rifled through or hurled into a passing garbage truck, my lunch money stolen, being shoved to the ground and the occasional stomach punch with its crumpling ache. Of them all, one incident remains vivid and self-defining.

I was twelve years old and walking to school one morning on West 106th Street on Manhattan's Upper West Side. As I turned the corner onto Broadway, my stomach flopped. A clutch of African American kids was hanging out in front of a candy store (which wasn't really a candy store because all they sold were tiny plastic bags of pot).

Before I could pivot, they'd spotted me—a short, pudgy, Jewish seventh grader in a bulky winter coat, weighed down by a backpack crammed full of books.

"Hey, check this out!" the tallest kid called. "The Master's little boy! What's in the bag, white boy?"

As they advanced, all I saw was a phalanx of cruel smiles, harsh laughter, and clenched fists. I'd been jumped by a gang of kids before, so I knew the script. And I knew where this gang got their inspiration.

That week, in January 1977, the country had been transfixed by the broadcast television miniseries, *Roots*. It was based on a best-selling book about slavery told from the African point of view, written by a Black man—author Alex Haley.

Dramatic scenes of the violence and hardships suffered at the hands of slave owners shocked TV audiences accustomed to more wholesome, nostalgic shows like *Little House on the Prairie* and *Happy Days*. For the time, the depictions of the brutality were graphic and cringeworthy. Viewers couldn't look away.

Roots had been a publishing sensation. The book perched for more than five months at the top of the *New York Times* bestseller list. In those three-channels-only, pre-cable days, the filmed version of a best-selling novel would have been expected to attract a large audience. *Roots* blew the doors off the hinges. By the final episode of the eight-night series, half of all the households in America had tuned in, and mine was no exception.

The *Roots* phenomenon blossomed into a social movement. In Black America it fired up interest in African American history and genealogy. In much of White America, it evoked a mix of empathy, curiosity, guilt, and not a little rage. *Roots* precipitated what some called "breakthrough" conversations—among coworkers, church members, in classrooms, and across millions of kitchen tables—about America's original sin.

The boys hovering over me that winter morning on upper Broadway had clearly been among the inspired. But I knew the only breakthrough in this conversation was going to be about me getting roughed up for the umpteenth time.

Ours was that sort of neighborhood in 1977—neglected, hostile, and often violent. New York City was, for all intents and purposes, bankrupt in those days. Broken streetlights stayed broken. Potholes sat empty and grew deeper. On warm days, the air was fetid with the stench of uncollected garbage. Drivers of New York's iconic yellow cabs—the safe ones that didn't cheat you—often refused fares above 96th Street because so many cabbies had been robbed in that part of the city.

On those mean streets I stood out as easy prey for muggers and bullies. I scurried to and from school and errands, constantly checking over my shoulders for potential threats, hugging the shadows to make myself as invisible as possible. I developed an instinct familiar to long-time city dwellers. Like a creature in the wild, all my senses were tuned to what was going on around me at all times, avoiding eye contact with strangers while surreptitiously assessing threats and planning escapes.

Such a visceral sense for danger also seemed to be baked into my Jewish DNA after thousands of years of attempts to eradicate our people. We memorialize that history of survival in our most sacred rituals—rituals my family observed with a real sense of devotion to tradition, even if we lacked a certain religious fervor. Keeping our Jewish traditions gave meaning to the lives of our relatives who perished in the Holocaust, and so we made a point of celebrating Shabbat every week as well as the holidays of Rosh Hashana, Yom Kippur, and Passover.

By fifth grade I knew by heart the Passover tale of the Israelites' suffering in Egypt as slaves under Pharaoh's heel, the parting of the Red Sea that allowed them to escape to freedom, and all the rest of it—the Jewish version of *Roots*. Now, just as those boys on Broadway were about to torment me on my way to school, something clicked.

"Wait!" I chirped. "I'm not white!"

The tall boy snorted. "Bullshit! You must really want an ass kicking!"

My chest tightened. I had to gulp for air.

"It's true!" I gasped. "I'm actually not white, I'm Jewish! ...And Jews were slaves too...in Egypt...you know, 'Let my people go'? ... It's all in the Bible! Honest!"

The group froze for an instant as they looked at each other with puzzled expressions. Then one of their faces lit up.

"Hey! That's right, man! I heard about that in church. Pharaoh made the Israelites slaves, and God punished the Egyptians by killing all their babies."

"Right!" another chimed. "That's when Moses parted the sea, right? Crazy!"

The tall boy who had started it all crossed his arms, cocked his head, and squinted at me. "Well, you're *still* white...but I guess you're okay. The Jews had it bad also." With that, the phalanx parted and let me go.

Trembling, I scampered off to school and safety. I was stunned by my miraculous escape and impressed by my powers of persuasion. Although I was too young to fully process the incident, the message was clear. I might never be able to fight my way out of a jam, but I now knew it was possible to talk my way out.

As a child, I wouldn't have guessed that I would grow up to become a rabbi. But by the time I faced that group of kids and found a way to connect with them and save myself from their wrath, I was already keenly interested in what it meant to be a Jew and in relating to the five-thousand-year-old story of my tribe. Like those kids on the corner, my identity was molded in part by something I'd seen on television years earlier—the news coverage of the Munich Massacre. That event was so disturbing and visceral that it jolted me out of the haze of childhood and set the compass for my future.

From that moment on, I developed a feeling of kinship with African Americans. Every year, our family's Passover seders fostered dialogue about all types of oppression. We would not only sing Jewish and Yiddish spirituals, but Black ones as well. In fact, at least half of the people who sat at our seder tables were not Jewish, and many of them were African American. We tried not to compare our oppressions but instead used our respective histories to understand one another.

Eventually, I would need to reconcile my intellectual understanding with my emotional history. I have always seen myself as an absolute fighter for equal rights for anyone and everyone, but the experience of having been mugged by young men of color created a bias for me that has had a lasting effect, both as a communal leader and within my own family as well.

* * *

Throughout high school, I continued to spend weekends with my father in Brooklyn. Every Saturday, we went to his small Orthodox synagogue for services. Although he technically belonged to a large Reform congregation, that was more of a practical membership—a means of making sure we could spend our summers swimming at the community pool. For Shabbat and holidays, he preferred the small, intimate service. At first, my father had to practically drag my brother and me out of bed every Saturday morning. What teenager wanted to get up to go to a three-hour service every week? I complained like crazy, but a part of me knew that I wanted to be there. It was foreign and familiar all at once. The tunes seemed to be ingrained in me from some place deep in my history, so that even though I didn't know Hebrew well enough to keep up with the words, they still felt relevant to me. Before long, I grew fond of the traditional prayer service myself and came to truly enjoy my time at the synagogue. I felt ill equipped, but at home. I watched everything that happened—the standing and sitting, small bows from the knee, swaying in time to the melodies. I plugged into the rhythms of the chanting. I listened to the rabbi's sermons, which made me wander into the crevices of my own soul. I began a quiet practice of talking to God, engaging in a silent, meditative conversation. The rabbi's words made me think deeply about the world and about why my life was unfolding in the ways that it was. I sat and listened to the elderly men reflect on their lives as they ate herring and drank scotch after the service.

Most of all, I loved talking to the rabbi. He was kind and patient and always encouraged me to ask more questions. He didn't care that I was fat or that I was lost in my parents' divorce. He lit up when I smiled. He cared about what I did and how I did it. Although he was traditional in his orthodoxy and wasn't interested in a progressive religious life, he didn't judge others for practicing Judaism differently. Without realizing it, he was guiding me toward a future career in the rabbinate, even though the branch of Judaism I would eventually choose was nothing like his own. Indeed, one day, he would proudly write a recommendation for me to go to a Reform rabbinical school. His acceptance was everything to me.

In those days, I wasn't much of a student. I eventually figured out that I was smart but not interested high school. At home, my parents cared about our education, but they were too busy trying to figure out how to put food on the table to spend much time noticing our grades. And so, I put in just enough effort to get Bs in classes that piqued my interest and Cs in the classes that didn't.

Needless to say, I didn't put too much time or energy into my college plans either. I would follow the path of least resistance and attend Hofstra University, where my father was a professor, and where tuition would be free. If, after one year, my grades were high enough and I'd found some direction for my studies, I'd consider transferring to another school. I was fine with this plan for a while, but in my senior year of high school, I decided that what I needed more than college was a break. This was my big moment of rebellion, or so I thought.

Instead of going to Hofstra, I wanted to put off college for a year and travel to Israel to live and work on a kibbutz. I assumed both my parents would be appalled at the idea of delaying my college admission and starting my journey to adulthood. Instead, they both agreed that this was a great plan. I was immature in those days and without much direction. A year of travel and new experiences would do me good, they ascended. Before I knew it, I was working odd jobs to save money for airfare and then I was on my way to Kibbutz Ma'ayan Tzvi, a place that was nothing more than a dot on a map to me at that time.

My year in Israel was formative to say the least. For the first three months, I was homesick and lonely. I barely spoke a word of Hebrew and everything was unfamiliar. Kibbutz life was rougher than I could have imagined, and I was given the unglamorous and physically challenging job of dishwasher, scouring pots and pans the size of an oven for hours a day. I graduated from washing pots and pans to picking cotton, caging turkeys, driving tractors, and mopping floors. Eventually I worked my way up to managing the dining hall. The hard, repetitive work resonated with me. In some ways, I found the menial jobs I did to be meditative, opening a path for inner reflection that reminded me of the time I spent at my dad's orthodox synagogue. I examined my life and realized it was time to take responsibility for how I presented myself to the world and to solidify my own unique connection to Judaism.

That year, I learned that it was possible to experience Judaism in a completely secular context. Only a handful of my fellow kibbutzniks celebrated Yom Kippur, which was shocking to me. They lived in the homeland and spoke Hebrew, and yet religious traditions were far from priorities. It was confusing to say the least, and I found myself writing letters to my Orthodox rabbi in Brooklyn, looking for a way to make sense of this spiritual identity crisis. In our correspondence, I learned to distinguish Zionism from Judaism, to accept this new perspective as valid and valiant. It was exhilarating for me to think so deeply about issues that meant so much to me, while literally living through my own version of the conversation in real time.

Being so far away from home, I was able to find some much needed distance from the toxicity of my childhood homes. Because making international calls was so prohibitively expensive in those days, I was not only physically distanced from home, but I had to go weeks without speaking to my parents for the first time in my life. I spoke to my mother on the first Sunday of every month, paying close attention to the time and calculating the bill in my head as the minutes ticked by. As a result of being so far away and so infrequently in touch with my own parents and siblings, I carved out a new community of friends who became my de facto Israeli family. Before long, I had fallen in love with the land, lost sixty pounds, and became fluent in Hebrew. I was so enamored with Israeli culture, Zionism, and my burgeoning Jewish identity that I never wanted to leave.

In America, I had always been a follower. A heavy-set kid who just wanted everyone in my family to get along, I was more than willing to go with the flow in order to avoid conflict. In Israel, with no one but myself to worry about, I blossomed into a leader. I learned a new language and found my voice.

Toward the end of my year in Israel, I called my mother for what was to be one of our last monthly phone calls. I told her I planned to make aliyah (to declare citizenship), join the Israeli army, and drop out of Hofstra before I'd even started. What followed was the biggest fight we've ever had. She demanded I come home, and I declared that I would not. We hung up without reaching a resolution.

That day, I went straight to my "Kibbutz Mother," the matriarch of the family I'd been paired with during my stay. We spoke (in Hebrew!) about the fight, and I waited for her to pat me on the back and congratulate me on my brave decision to leave home for good and join our people in Israel. Instead, she curtly told me, in her no-nonsense Israeli manner, that mothers were more important than Zionism (or at least equal in value), and it was time for me to go home. I was crushed but somehow suddenly compliant. There must have been something waiting for me back in the United States, I assumed, something I couldn't yet imagine.

Two weeks later, I was back in New York, registering for college classes.

* * *

Back in America, it took me some time to find my grounding again. Much of my early college experience was aimless. I needed five years to graduate from Hofstra because I changed my major so many times—I started out pre-med, then moved to business, and finally settled on political science. I went from girlfriend to girlfriend, and I partied with my friends and my fraternity brothers. But once I homed in on my final major, things started to fall into place for me.

I loved politics. I watched debates the way other people watched the World Series. It was an intellectual sport, and I wanted to play all the time. Declaring my (final) major as Political Science finally felt right. I loved my classes and felt more engaged in them than I had in so many others. My grades improved quickly now that I was finally excited about my studies.

One of my clearest memories from those years was when I went head-to-head with the "chief class conservative." I can't quite remember what we were arguing about, but I know I used every possible liberal sound bite to put my classmate in his place. He was enraged as he touted the virtues of the Reagan presidency.

"The president created millions of jobs, turned the economy around, and brought respect back to the reputation of the United States of America," he fervently declared.

I laughed, knowing I was a better speaker, more passionately connected to what it meant to be "right." And I instinctively spouted back my pithy arguments of passion, "But your president is a war monger who simply strong-arms the Soviet enemy, portraying strength that's just bravado; all of which could end up in mutual destruction."

Our professor let the argument go on a few minutes before telling us to settle down. He allowed a few other students to join in and take sides. Many of the other students agreed with me because in the mid-1980s on Long Island, most of them were instinctively left.

I felt good about myself. I liked being right. I liked being supported by my classmates. And I could tell that the professor was a liberal, and therefore he had to be on my side.

Instead, Professor Levantrosser, a humble and bright man, sighed in disappointment and said, chidingly, "Dear students, I am always up for a substantive political debate. Our democracy was built on pointed disagreements. But a word to the wise...perhaps some of you should read your chapters as passionately as you argue in class. If you matched your zeal for argumentation with substance and preparation, you would argue with something more worthwhile."

I froze in my chair. He was talking about me. He knew an unprepared student a mile away. I fooled most of my classmates, but I was running on emotion alone with no academic substance to back it up. The Conservative student wasn't as loud or as charismatic as I was, but he knew more about what he was talking about than I did.

This experience taught me I'd better prepare more for class, but it also made me wonder why I felt so comfortable and passionate about my political leanings without believing I needed to know more about the substance behind them. Generally, one feels confident about matters in life because of study or experience. I remained absolutely sure of my positions, but I realized I still needed to learn about both sides of any issue I was going to debate. Perhaps more importantly, I discovered that other people out there had legitimate points of view that differed from my own, and I just might learn a thing or two if I listened to them.

As that young man who arrived at political science class in the mid-1980s, I was motivated to fight for my beliefs. They had been formed by good people, family, and clergy, who wanted me to do right in the world. My learning process until then was based more on emotion and passion than on knowledge about policy. This is not unusual. After all, how many parents take the time to explain the details of their political positions to their children— let alone those of the opposite party? Most of us inherit what we were taught, and what I was taught was ethical and good—it just didn't always allow for other shades of truth or different points of view that were also ethical in nature but didn't arrive at the same place. I had learned that doing right was good, but I was never taught that there can be many paths to the same end.

As I have grown and matured, I've come to see that no one owns the truth. There are certain "red lines" that no human being should cross, but most of the rest of the world is painted in shades of gray. For a long time, I lived in a world where things were either black or white, correct or incorrect, good or evil. That worked as long as I surrounded myself with people who thought the same way I did. Perhaps that afternoon, in my political science class, I started to wake up to a new and unfolding reality.

* * *

Like many recent graduates, I had no idea what to do with my life when I finished my degree at Hofstra. Going into politics was an exciting prospect but one I didn't feel ready for just yet. Plus, I had rent to pay in Manhattan. And so, I took my degree and applied for practical jobs that had nothing to do with my studies. I ended up working as an Operations Manager Trainee at Chubb, a large insurance company.

At the time, I was pulling in $26,000 a year, which was not quite enough to support myself in the city. Fortunately, I'd already been teaching Hebrew school at a local synagogue for several years in college, a job one of my fraternity brothers suggested for me since my Hebrew was so solid after my time in Israel. It was one of those jobs I'd never envisioned for myself but one that fit naturally into the rhythm of my life. I loved the students and really enjoyed my time with them on Tuesday and Thursday evenings and Sunday mornings. Even though those extra teaching hours meant that I needed to stay up even later to get my classwork done, I soon found myself volunteering to run youth group activities as well.

So when I started working at Chubb and found that I still needed extra cash to make ends meet in the city, I kept working at the Hebrew school as well. This was great not only because I needed the supplemental income but because working with those kids and spending time in a synagogue setting was deeply meaningful to me. I was not trained to be a teacher, but I was raised by two parents who both taught professionally. It almost felt like it was in my DNA. I knew instinctively from my own lackluster school experience that if I didn't make the material relevant to those kids, they wouldn't have a reason to make an effort to learn.

Instead of teaching to their brains, I'd teach to their hearts. We would read textbook chapters and then find ways to connect that information to them personally.

The kids took to me because I didn't talk down to them. We spoke openly about the difficulties of being a teenager, about their hobbies and interests, and issues that were important to them. As I got to know them, our class became as much about emotional intelligence as it did about academics. And once they were comfortable with me, the really deep learning began to take place. As a kid who never loved school myself, I found tremendous value in becoming the kind of teacher I wished I could have had. I may not have known how to present the curriculum in a traditional way, but somehow it worked for me, and every time I'd come home from Religious School I felt I'd done something good in the world. This was not something I could say about my day job. I was only twenty-two at the time, and so in some ways I wasn't really expecting professional fulfillment, but I did realize that something was missing for me in the business world.

My mother asked me to come see her on the first Yom Kippur of my post-college life, and I left services with my father to go pay her a visit in the city. What she told me then was really unexpected. She believed children knew a lot more about themselves than adults gave them credit for. I agreed. She made it a practice to ask young children about their career aspirations because they were often more insightful than you would guess. I agreed with that assertion also. I had no idea where she was going with this until she started to tell one of those famous bits of family lore that always made us laugh at holiday gatherings. When I was five years old, I declared that I wanted to be a rabbi on a motorcycle.

But today, she wasn't looking for a nostalgic laugh. She was worried about me and sensed that although I was content in my life, I wasn't fulfilled. She had decided that I should become a rabbi after all.

My mother was serious, but I laughed out loud. What an absurd idea! I was a young guy who liked to party with his friends till all hours of the morning. I couldn't keep a girlfriend for more than a few weeks, and I enjoyed eating all kinds of non-kosher foods. I was definitely not rabbi material!

Or was I?

I loved my side job as a Hebrew school teacher and youth group leader. Connecting with those kids was the highlight of my week. And I had always excelled at public speaking and debate, defending my ideas and beliefs in general. At home, I was the one who could speak to both sides of the family and broker peace when there was so much disagreement. Come to think of it, I had been the kind of kid who could talk himself out of being mugged—and teach a lesson at the same time! And my time in Israel remained the highlight of my young life, an experience I thought about every single day.

Still, when I went home that night and told my roommate about this conversation, I was sure to let him know I thought my mother was completely insane. He didn't laugh. Actually, he agreed with her and said of course this was what I should be doing—wasn't it obvious? The next day I brought it up with the principal of the Hebrew school at which I taught, and she also agreed that this would be a great plan for me. I couldn't believe it—they were all out of their minds!

For the next three years, I continued to dismiss the thought of becoming a rabbi. There were bigger and better things to do. More women to date, more money to make, more socializing to do in the city. But sooner or later, I knew that I wanted more out of my life. I wanted a job that I couldn't leave behind at my desk at 5:00 p.m. I wanted a life that was richer and deeper, one that would touch the lives of others. So I began to take my mother's advice seriously and look into the idea of rabbinical school.

In the end, it was the rabbi from my supplemental job at the synagogue who convinced me to apply to the Hebrew Union College–Jewish Institute of Religion. His argument was, in a nutshell: "What have you got to lose? You can always go back to business if this doesn't work out, and—worst case scenario—you gain a master's degree and round out your Jewish education."

I knew I wasn't the ideal candidate. My future classmates had attended the best Ivy League schools and already had solid backgrounds in Jewish studies. Besides my high level of spoken Hebrew, I didn't think I had much to offer to the school. To be honest, going to rabbinical school was more of a gut decision than an intellectual one. I was still engaging in my private practice of speaking to God, and something about being in dialogue with a higher being gave me solace and confidence when things were stressful. With my friends, I could always talk for hours about philosophy. But could I turn that private interest and introspection into a career?

I decided to take my chances and enroll. One of the very first things I did as a rabbinical student was to begin seeing a therapist. My mother had encouraged me to find someone to help me deal with the scars of my childhood, and now the time seemed right to do so. At first, I wasn't sure this was something I would enjoy. Dredging up pain from the past and talking about uncomfortable situations in the present didn't exactly seem like a fun way to spend even one hour a week.

But my mentors encouraged it, and in fact, the seminary offered to pay for the first ten sessions for any student who wanted to try, because they knew rabbis, like all faith leaders, carry a heavy burden. They explained that it would be a good idea for me to learn how to deal with the emotional toll of the difficult times my congregants were experiencing with a neutral third party rather than with my future wife and kids. Furthermore, understanding my own psychological baggage could only aid me in helping others to deal with their own. This was one of the best decisions I have made, and ever since, I have always been actively in therapy.

My first of five years in rabbinical school would be spent in Jerusalem. The chance to spend substantive time in the place where I thrived most as a human being filled me with excitement. But the learning of scripture and other ancient Jewish texts was a less enthralling prospect. What if it was all boring, more academic than spiritual? And how would my classmates turnout to be? I fully admit that at the time, I had a rather stereotypical image of what a rabbi would be like—nerdy, out of touch with sports and popular culture, and so forth.

I arrived in Israel with all my physical and emotional baggage in tow. My goodness, did I have a lot to learn about rabbinic studies and the people who engaged with them. I found my classmates to be well-rounded, interesting, relevant, smart, compassionate, and generous souls. Their interests and talents were likewise varied and complex, as were their personalities. Far from the monolith I'd expected, my classmates were athletes, comedians, academics, artists, and philosophers. To this day, the fifty students who made up our class all have a special place in my heart. I'm closer with some than with others, and there have been conflicts over the years, but the bond we have shared over the last twenty-five years will always remain strong. The common thread that bound us together that year was our desire to make the world a better place and to share our faith in a higher power.

Unlike other denominations of Judaism, students admitted to Reform rabbinical seminaries have vastly different levels of Jewish education. Some, like me, were competent in Hebrew, while others were beginners. Some had a strong background in biblical and rabbinic texts; some had much to learn. This made for a rich and complex learning environment with a many-layered curriculum. Indeed, over five years of study, students must become proficient in traditional Hebrew, enough to learn all of the traditional texts in the ancient language itself as well as professional rabbinics. Homiletics, counseling, officiation at lifecycle events, oration, theology, ethics, and liturgy were all part of our studies. It was a lot. Beyond our classwork, we all had to serve in internships to gain real life rabbinic experiences.

There were plenty of moments of doubt as I began my studies, but soon I found my place and adjusted to the pace and breadth of my studies. I especially loved studying Bible and Jewish law. My head and heart became connected through my studies in ways that had previously eluded me. It wasn't easy to balance it all, especially since I hadn't taken academics seriously in my life to this point. I knew I felt a spiritual calling but wondered if I would be able to articulate that calling to future congregants. One of our professors told us, "Every rabbi only preaches one sermon their whole life. They just come at it in different ways." For the next few years, it would be my job to begin to articulate my essential message as a spiritual leader.

It was in Eugene Borowitz's theology class that I realized rabbinical school would indeed combine so many of my passions—debate, politics, and history—and sharpen my skills in all of them such that I could make this career a reality. It was here that I would finally learn the substance of the arguments I loved to make so passionately.

Rabbi Borowitz was tough. He didn't pass students from his class unless we could substantively articulate our ideas and thoughts about God, afterlife, theodicy, and ethics. He forced us to think like I was never made to think before. He made us write and re-write papers until our thoughts were cohesive and clear. He didn't let us hide; he made sure that we developed the rabbinic chops to serve our people and be able to entertain the most complicated existential questions. When I passed Rabbi Borowitz's muster, I started to believe that my calling to God was indeed my vocation for life.

When I was a kid in the 1970s, organized religion in general was hierarchical and emotionally sterile. Even well into my twenties, especially in suburban synagogues, too many rabbis were autocrats. Those were the days when rabbis talked *at* you rather than *to* you, and they determined the experience you would have at their synagogue rather than asking for your opinion. They were the experts, and they did not leave room for interpretation.

When I decided to become a rabbi, I was determined not to be an unrelatable scholar who always had his nose in the Talmud. I played and loved sports, and I enjoyed nights out in the city. When my fellow students and I went out drinking, they'd sometimes tell girls that they were in medical or law school. Doctors and lawyers were sexy. Being a rabbi? *Meh!* But I was never embarrassed to tell the truth. I was going to be a rabbi who was just as in touch with the current culture as with Jewish tradition. I might never become the rabbi on a gleaming motorcycle I'd imagined in childhood, but I would become a rabbi, just as my five-year-old self had predicted.

CHAPTER THREE:

For the Sake of Heaven

J ewish history has had more than its share of nightmarish periods. One of the worst goes back to the destruction of the Second Temple in Jerusalem in 70 CE and the fall of the last sovereign Jewish state to precede the one we know today. The Roman enemy was indeed powerful, but according to the Talmud, the philosophical and perhaps most significant reason for their defeat was senseless hatred among the Jewish people themselves, a state of mind that comes about when people stop talking to one another like human beings. Arguments and civil discourse have always been hallmarks of Jewish living, sewn into the fabric of Jewish traditional texts. The allure of being Jewish is intimately connected to the ability and obligation to healthily argue, dismantle, and unpack ideas, so that each person can learn and grow from the other. Without that ability, we devolve as a society.

The Talmud, the second major body of Jewish Law, is written in the form of dueling opinions. The narrative almost never begins with a legal opinion, but instead with several points of view, representing whole and divergent schools of thought. This is to remind us that when we study, we aren't just looking for the answer to complex questions, as opposed to the spirit and evolution of the argument. The scholars-of-old beg us to dig into the dichotomy of their thoughts so we can build the same in ourselves. This healthy discourse exists not simply to arrive at an answer, but to build the multi-layered and complicated fiber of people and the community in which they live. In seminary, we often learn in pairs of two, called *chevruta*, studying the same text in tandem and practicing the art of playing devil's advocate to one's study partner, together exploring the nuances of the material. This uniquely Jewish form of debate is called *"machloket,"* which I translate as "argument for the sake of heaven."

Two thousand years ago in the Jewish empire, people stopped wanting to argue or listen to other points of view and instead gave in to the human tendency toward hubris and arrogance, pride and laziness. To be "right" was to be mighty. There are countless texts in the Talmud about communities devolving when people dug into their own beliefs and biases rather than communicating and debating with one another. Story after story describes senseless arguments "in the name of God" that resulted in murder and violence. Jewish texts warned the people time and again, but to no avail, and history continued to repeat itself.

Rather than strengthen us, this attitude of absolutism built walls of intolerance between people who were supposed to live, learn, and grow together. Before long, hatred became so enmeshed in the communal fabric that when this society was called upon to fight a common enemy, there was simply no cohesion or will to do so. And the rabbis explain that this was how the Jewish empire was lost.

Winning a war takes military might, but it also takes a communal heart that believes in its core values and holds a commitment to its national interests. When that is lost, there is no way to rally around one another to defeat an enemy. The Romans may have been the ones who physically defeated the Jewish state, but it was ready for the taking because of the pervasive animosity of one citizen for another.

That story sends a chill down my spine to this day. When I first learned about it in rabbinical school, it inspired me to do my part in creating a cohesive, functioning Jewish community that could withstand pressures from the outside world. Beyond the logistics of training rabbis for future careers at the pulpit, rabbinical school is about creating a group of peers whose relationships will evolve over a lifetime of shared study, intellectual development, and communal leadership. As students, we spent years engaging in the Talmudic notion of *machloket*, sure that the very act of arguing with each other was for the betterment of the cosmic ether. The theory is that through disagreement and sacred discourse the deepest of connections are formed, and one's character is strengthened so that it's possible to stay strong in the face of enmity.

Machloket, so akin to the debates I loved in college, was perhaps my favorite aspect of my course of study, and the one that would stay with me the longest as I developed my rabbinic career. Engaging in vigorous debate, we students were able to reveal layers of our own truths—to display the subtlety each of us has to offer without sacrificing our friendship or mutual respect. We would argue about such ethical issues as when a dying patient might be taken off life support, or how to practice ancient Jewish rituals in modern times, such as dietary restrictions or Sabbath and other Jewish holiday observance.

Seminary gave me the freedom to come into my classes and present my perspective on the world and to be critiqued by my professors and peers when the stakes were still relatively low. During these formative years, I was able to try out ideas and watch as they were either vehemently denied or encouraged and lifted up.

As we progressed through our studies over the years, we tried to be open to the possibility of incorporating other points of view into our deeply personal, deeply ingrained philosophies. One way to encourage this broadening of our minds was to be sent to small student pulpits or to internships in large congregations throughout the country for real-time experience. Some of my classmates were placed in synagogues as far flung as rural New Hampshire, North Carolina, and Pennsylvania, where surely they would have to be open to new perspectives and life experiences.

I, however, landed a mile from where I grew up in New York City, at Congregation Rodeph Sholom. A vibrant, two-thousand-family congregation on the Upper West Side, Rodeph Sholom would be my home for the next thirteen years, as I was fortunate enough to be hired there after my internship ended and I was ordained from the Hebrew Union College-Jewish Institute of Religion, the Reform Rabbinic Seminary.

Rodeph Sholom was a hub of intellectual, and spiritual activity. Worship services drew five hundred to eight hundred members weekly for Sabbath Services, while adult learning classes happened regularly and were well attended. Social life for our members revolved around the congregation. People met each other at Temple and were then connected in activities organized by the synagogue or by virtue of the relationships built on their own. People who belonged there were typically at the top of their respective fields, and often our congregants themselves or their esteemed colleagues would offer classes, lectures, or guest sermons.

Besides a religious school of five hundred children, which is customary for any reform synagogue, there was also a successful and vibrant day school, in which children received both their secular and Jewish education during each school day. Day schools are much more prominent in the conservative and orthodox wings of Jewish denominational life, but only about twenty exist in the Reform Movement. Generally, Reform families feel that a few hours a week of religious education is sufficient for their children's spiritual upbringing, but Rodeph Sholom's day school has been thriving as one of the better schools in the very competitive private school environment of New York City for almost fifty years.

As one of the largest congregations in the country, with three rabbis, two cantors, and several interns, Rodeph Sholom was also one of the most innovative Temples of the 1990s. At a time when many Christians walked away from their churches as the religious right became more vocal in national politics, religiously liberal Jews also began to give up their synagogue connections. They saw the literalism of conservative religion as an affront to their modern sensibilities while at the same time they were lost in a spiritual wilderness without a healthy sense of inner meaning and purpose.

To combat that unfortunate combination, we made huge efforts to develop positive associations with religious practice, leaning heavily on the powerful desire our congregants had for social action. This experience of Jewish spirituality as both traditional religious experience and social activism worked well. Membership was bursting at the seams, and our youth program was packed with kids hungry to learn and incorporate Judaism into their already hectic lives. It was a renaissance of sorts, and I felt lucky to be a part of it at such an early point in my career.

These were years of rapid professional growth, and I was blessed to be working under the tutelage of senior Rabbi Robert N. Levine, one of the finest mentors and rabbis in the country, and other clergy and staff who kept me on my toes and made sure I was reaching to produce superlative work. In those early years of my career, I always tried to remember the lesson of the Temple's destruction and make sure that I engaged in respectful debate with my colleagues and congregants whenever possible. But to be honest, in those thirteen years, the opportunities to debate someone whose ideas were truly different from my own were few and far between.

During my tenure at Rodeph Sholom, from 1997 to 2006, roughly one of every ten members was a Republican; the majority were proudly Democratic. Although in years past there had been many prominent New York Jewish Republicans, including admired figures like Senator Jacob Javits, the trend was now firmly liberal. Democratic Congressman Jerrold Nadler represented our district in the US Congress, and he won every election by an average of sixty points. If people voted Republican, they certainly didn't advertise it. At most, some (particularly those who worked in banking and finance) would say that they were fiscally conservative, but that was about the extent of it. The names Ronald Reagan and George Bush were almost curse words in our community, and favoring conservative policies like welfare reform, opposition to abortion, or the so-called War on Drugs was out of the question. Most people who lived on New York's Upper West Side proudly branded themselves old-time lefties—and still do.

On the one hand, this was an amazing time and place to be surrounded by liberal values. The commitment to fixing our broken world was palpable, and our synagogue was an epicenter for balancing the scales of justice. We started and ran a nightly men's homeless shelter. Our congregants provided nightly meals, and two members slept over with the men to provide fellowship, support, and care every night, including the holidays. We collected ten to twenty thousand pounds of food for the hungry every High Holy Day season, and coats in the winter for those who were cold. Every month, our lobby collection bins were filled to the brim with diapers, shoes, notebooks, backpacks, and gently used sports equipment. Our congregation gave and did anything we felt we could give and do for those who suffered in our midst.

We took our teens through the streets of Manhattan to give out these items in person, so our children could absorb the moral imperative of making our world a better place for anyone and everyone. We reached out to our African American brothers and sisters to promote interracial community through Passover seders, joint worship services, and pulpit exchanges. We believed that fostering a religious environment meant making our world a kinder and more compassionate place. I was proud to be a rabbi of a synagogue where significant commitments were made to better our community.

Yet, this philosophy of doing good became clouded when it was conflated with political policy. Assumptions were made that fixing the world was something the Democratic Party alone was able to do. No one said this overtly, but it was clear that most of our congregants felt Democrats were the ones who stood for improving the nature of the world, while Republicans were motivated by self-interest in the spirit of free market capitalism. Members of our social action committee referred to Republicans in Washington, DC, as Neanderthals, and if such a remark was challenged, their response was, "When Republicans start acting differently, we will refer to them differently." The GOP's bur-geoning association with the Christian right during these years did not help matters with liberal Jews.

When Ronald Reagan died in 2004, my senior rabbi men-tioned him before our congregation recited our weekly memo-rial prayer, but he did so apologetically, as if merely speaking his name was offensive. When this came up the next day in a class I taught, I too apologized. And yet, in retrospect, I didn't quite understand the problem our senior rabbi had caused. We had such a low opinion of Reagan's presidency that paying him honor when he died needed to come with a qualifying apology. To me, there was nothing odd about this fact.

Our behavior was reinforced by the echo chamber of beliefs in which we all existed and which so many of us reaffirmed daily. Even as a leader of the community, I failed to see that some of my congregants might be offended by our apology because they authentically considered Reagan a good president whose policy positions they endorsed, particularly his anti-communism and support for Israel. It simply didn't occur to me to factor in this possibility, because the overwhelming majority of people in our community thought and voted the way I did. I never paused to consider the conflict I might have been causing in my own congregation by ignoring these minority points of view.

* * *

During my years at Rodeph Sholom, the cultural landscape of America was shifting dramatically, but it was harder to shift my own perspective than I might have guessed. One issue in particular taught me that if I wanted to lead my own congregation someday, I would have to work harder to embrace those congregants whose ideas conflicted with mine. Unexpectedly, it was a conversation with one of our straight, Republican congregants at a Shabbat dinner for gay and lesbian community members that helped me realize I was not as "inclusive" as I thought.

In the 1990s, debates over officiation of intermarriage and gay marriage were hotly contested in rabbinic circles. Today, amongst liberal clergy, this is not much of an argument, but twenty-plus years ago, a majority of clergy would not officiate at either. Indeed, those were the early years in which seminaries were just beginning to ordain openly gay and lesbian rabbis.

I mentioned earlier that my parents divorced when I was ten. What I didn't know then, and wouldn't know for many years to come, was that my mother came out to her social circle as a lesbian after the divorce. We kids were not informed because back then, in the mid-1970s, my mother worried that we might be bullied or, worst of all, taken away from her. It's hard to believe now, but less than fifty years ago, she could have been declared unfit by the state and stripped of her parental rights because of her sexual orientation. A few decades later, my older sister would also come out as gay. So for me, discussions about gay and lesbian rights and inclusion in synagogue culture were tinged with deeply personal feelings about some of my closest family members. I had much to say about this issue, and I was absolutely sure that only liberal Democrats were LGBTQ+ allies.

For all our activism and political posturing, when it came to accepting and embracing the LGBTQ+ community, we had a long way to go in 1994 when I was still an intern and there was a rabbinic opening at Rodeph Sholom. The committee searched for months until we fell in love with an incredibly talented young rabbi. She was smart, sensitive, articulate, caring, innovative, and confident. She could serve all ages and stages of our congregation. As she entered the final round of the interview process, she told the committee she was a lesbian. She didn't want us to discover that fact after she had been hired, and she wanted to live her life authentically rather than hide her identity. And so, we were faced with the decision of whether or not to hire one of the very first openly gay rabbis in the country.

I am sorry to say this wasn't a decision our hiring committee came to lightly. She was unquestionably the best candidate for the position. But we were in relatively uncharted waters. At that time, there was only one openly gay rabbi in America. Until then, the rabbinate operated under a kind of "don't ask don't tell" policy, and gay rabbis would be forced to either hide their personal lives from their congregations or find a position outside of the pulpit. Things would shift dramatically in the years to come, but at the time, we were taking a huge leap of faith and making a tremendous statement when we decided, after much deliberation, to offer her the position.

Some committee members were absolutely uncomfortable with the decision, but they didn't say anything out loud because expressing such a sentiment when you lived on the Upper West Side of Manhattan would be seen as inappropriate, and they didn't want to be looked down upon. Ultimately, we decided that hiring her and helping to set the precedent for openness and trust in the community was more important than any conflict we might endure as a result.

I was personally overjoyed and felt that I was going to be her biggest ally, since I was so personally connected to the LGBTQ community. I was especially proud of Rabbi Levine, who actually put his career on the line by letting the committee know that if the candidate's sexual orientation proved to be the reason she wasn't offered the position, he would no longer be comfortable serving as the spiritual leader of the congregation. He put his livelihood and one of the most influential pulpits in America on the line for this moral imperative. Talk about being a rabbinic exemplar.

Before long, however, I found myself in a sticky situation. This new rabbi was confident and bold, and she wanted to make advances for other gay and lesbian clergy while also helping the congregation serve as a sanctuary for openly gay and lesbian families. She asked us to start a Gay and Lesbian Concerns Committee to integrate gays and lesbians into the congregation.

We were all on board with that, and we made it happen. But for her, that also included same-sex wedding officiation.

Same-sex weddings were not even close to being legal in any state at this time, and very few clerics were officiating at religious ceremonies for gay and lesbian couples. Even religiously liberal congregations had trouble seeing past the scriptural dictum, which stated that gay and lesbian life was forbidden. Whether they used the scripture as an excuse for their own personal discomfort or whether they truly took those words literally was almost beside the point. To officiate at gay weddings was to put your rabbinic career in jeopardy, and it was far from common practice.

For better or worse, the new rabbi decided to bring up the issue of officiating at gay weddings just a few years after starting her job at Rodeph Sholom. I myself was only six months into my official post there, and I had my whole career looming in front of me. This was an unusual situation to be sure, because such complex and controversial issues are generally not up for debate so early in a rabbi's tenure. She didn't yet have the trust of the congregation, something which is built slowly over many years of service and relationship. However, this topic was of such prominent and immediate concern to her that she forced the issue and brought it before the community in a clear and direct attempt to change the rules and set a new standard of inclusion for our community.

I will never forget that meeting, so long as I live. The committee summoned every member of the clergy and asked us to publicly declare if we would or would not officiate at gay weddings. Scores of people showed up to hear what we would say. I was terrified. So early on in my career, this was a moment that could have potentially changed the course of the rest of my life, starting right here at my very first synagogue posting.

Ethically, religiously, and otherwise, my mind was made up. I believed whole-heartedly in officiating at gay and lesbian marriages. I thought of my mother and sister and all the experiences they had endured through the years in order to live their authentic lives. It was abundantly clear to me that everyone, regardless of who they love, deserved the right to be married to that person, and if the government wouldn't allow it, certainly their religious institutions should. But I was young, and I'd barely had time to find my footing in the rabbinate. This issue was so fraught, and I could see that there were congregants who truly had never grappled with the questions before us. This rabbi had come into our lives and immediately shaken up the dynamic of a congregation that was unprepared for so much change so soon. They needed time to think things through and giving them a quick "yes" or "no" was not going to cut it.

For some time, the Committee had been hosting gay and lesbian Sabbath dinners for Jews of all denominations. They were astoundingly successful, with larger and larger crowds each time and citywide notoriety, especially in the LGBTQ+ community. However, our own gay members knew that real progress would come only if straight allies attended the dinners as well.

One night I was seated next to another straight congregant, who also happened to be a Republican. He quipped, "Isn't it interesting, Rabbi, when you look at all of the straight members here tonight, how many of them are Republicans?"

I hadn't been checking political affiliations at the door, but he was correct. He went on to say that liberal Democrats in the congregation talked a big game, but when it came to showing up to support the very issues they apparently held dear, they were nowhere to be found. I replied that he was reading too much into the attendance at this particular dinner, but he insisted I was missing a more substantive point. He felt that his Republican positions were dismissed out of hand in disparaging ways that were perhaps antithetical to what it means to be a Reform Jew.

He suggested that perhaps the congregation's Democrats subscribed philosophically to the Jewish liberal call because it got them accepted into the upper ranks of American Jewish life. They were what he described as "limousine liberals," people who spoke arrogantly of supporting justice and mercy without wanting to touch these incendiary issues themselves. He claimed they did not want what they supported, in this case gay rights, to ever touch their personal lives.

As a rabbi, I did not encourage his disparaging of the "other," especially using such derogatory language, but his suggestion that being a Republican was not as monolithic as some members of our community assumed hit home. After all, here he was, giving his in-person support of an issue many of the Democrats among us had advocated for, but had failed to show up for in real time. That interaction taught me that not only are there many shades of truth, but we must do better to learn from those whose truths are different from our own. He reminded me of the value of *makhloket*, of engaging with others in difficult conversations in order to learn and grow, which had been so dear to me in my rabbinical school years and beyond.

With this conversation in mind, I told the committee that I couldn't give them a "yes or no" answer on the spot that night.

Rather, it seemed to me that we as a congregation needed time to explore the issues, learn the texts, and debate the pros and cons of officiating at gay weddings before making such a groundbreaking change in our practice. There was so much at stake for me professionally that even though my heart urged me to embrace the opportunity to say yes and change my little corner of the world for the better right away, I knew I needed to take a step back and go slowly if I hoped to truly affect lasting change in the congregation.

After much reflection, I asked for a six-month period to study the issue alongside the congregants and come to my decision with their help. Clearly, there was a lot of work to be done to prepare our community for this kind of change, and that was not going to happen overnight. In retrospect, I feel proud of my younger self for somehow finding the kind of wisdom I haven't always shown in other times of my career. And yet, that night I was simply wracked with guilt and a degree of shame. I thought I had betrayed myself, my family, and every gay and lesbian person who deserved every right that I enjoyed as a straight man. I felt crushed, weak, and embarrassed.

I remember getting into an empty elevator as quickly as I could and bursting into tears once the meeting had ended. How would I face my mother and sister? I left the temple that night and went to get a drink to calm down. Then I called my mother and sister, explained what had taken place, and told them how sorry I was. I felt that I'd been cowardly. Was asking for six months to deliberate a sign of weakness and a signal to the community that my alliance with the gay community wasn't as strong as I thought it was? Should I have stood up and strongly affirmed my intention to officiate at gay weddings then and there? Was I just worried about my own career, putting my job ahead of my values?

To the contrary, they told me they couldn't be prouder. They said we would be better off if we created more allies through loving and patient teaching than through sheer authority. "Bring people along," they said. "Make sure you treat good people who just need to learn with the love and respect they deserve. Give them a safe space to ask questions and understand more deeply. Otherwise, you will turn them off forever."

For the next six months, I did my best to make my mother and sister proud, and to show patience for my members who really wanted to learn, to search their souls and figure out why gay marriage was so difficult for them to accept. It wasn't my job as a rabbi to shove ethics down their throats, but it was my responsibility to escort them in a learning process that would be thorough and non-judgmental. Of course, there were some people who were truly intolerant who would not agree to learn about or explore this topic. But for those who were simply lacking a background and looking for solid ground on which to make their decision, this extended period gave them the time they needed to adjust their mindsets and come to an informed decision.

Six months later, I declared officially and publicly that I would officiate at gay weddings. Not everyone came along. Some ended up being, in my mind, just as intolerant at the end of six months as they had been at the start. Given how unlikely it was that anyone in the community openly took scripture as the literal truth, I felt their stance was likely more about their own discomfort with homosexuality than it was about God and religion. But most people, when given the time to ask questions and study and engage with one another in debate, did come around. This learning process, though fraught with the possibility of cracking open the community, did the opposite. It brought people together to learn about themselves and their religious tradition in ways we never thought possible.

I am proud to say that as a result of this experience, I had the good fortune of being the first rabbi in the congregation's then one-hundred-sixty-year history to officiate at a gay wedding.

This early experience demonstrated what it means for people to engage in *makhloket* in the real world, to pull back from their instinctive anger and resentment toward those with different opinions and be present in the dialectic long enough to see the other side. We are entitled to our fears of the unknown, but real progress will come only when we allow ourselves to sit with others and navigate those fears, making sure we discern fear from actual intolerance. I was and will always be open to thoughtful opposition. But, after long and thorough discussion, people "just not being comfortable" was not something that felt acceptable to me.

I have found that most people's opposition to hot-button issues stems from a fear of the unknown combined with a lack of knowledge. When we give those people a chance to openly express their doubts and biases, and when we give them the respect they deserve as members of our sacred community, we allow them the space they need to consider other points of view.

If clerics are able to play the role of honest brokers, religious institutions can serve as a safe place to hold good-faith discussions. Unfortunately, it seems to me, too often they try to manipulate tradition to prove their political point. This is something all of us are guilty of from time to time, whether Christians, Jews, or Muslims. Once religion is used as a proof-text to push or guilt members into voting a specific way, the cleric loses his or her ability to bring good faith people of all stripes into a dialogue. When handled well, these discussions forge deep and abiding relationships, as well as ethical and moral imperatives that can direct us to discern between a religious ethical imperative and voting for a specific political party. Justice may take a bit longer to achieve, but if we find a place to sit down and have real conversations, we may achieve a longer lasting and more cemented connection of community and justice.

What can be worse than a preacher getting on a moral high horse and telling the congregation that he or she knows exactly what God wants from them? Almost any preacher with knowledge of the scripture can use the text to back up their specific policy position. Different religious denominations interpret scripture in varying ways. More orthodox denominations tend to follow the word of scripture as the letter of the law, while denominations that are more religiously liberal function more from the spirit of the word.

Our community was fairly monolithic in its view that justice would be achieved through liberal political thought, and it was hard to even recognize the isolation of those who thought differently. Although I believe this was not malicious in nature, many of us truly internalized the idea that there was only one real road to being just, and that was the road through which the Democratic party led. Every once in a while, a congregant complained that we didn't take him seriously because he was a Republican. Or, another said she didn't understand why the Religious Action

Center, the advocacy arm of the Reform movement, didn't take all members into account when postulating its political positions. To the mainstream congregant, and to members of the clergy, these complaints felt like a result of failing to "see the light" rather than legitimate arguments based on thoughtful consideration.

When the issue of gay and lesbian weddings arose, and I found myself in dialogue with people who had far different beliefs than my own but who nonetheless showed up to support and encourage people who felt isolated and alienated from the community, things began to shift for me. Until then, I was perfectly content to stay safe in my liberal cocoon, doling out definitive opinions without taking the time or making the effort to truly consider the substance of my arguments. While I appreciated the intellectual exercise of *makhloket*, until then, I hadn't had many opportunities to see it played out in real time with real-life consequences. I had a long way to go until I truly came into my own as a rabbi, but I was on my way, and I was excited to see what lay ahead for me outside of my safety zone.

CHAPTER FOUR:

A Day that Changed a Generation

On September 11, 2001, I was barely four years into my rabbinate and still learning the basics. In those early years, I was writing out sermons like term papers, collecting research, ruminating on big topics, formulating my opinions. Like schoolteachers who hone their lesson plans over the years, rabbis have to build up a reservoir of ideas and concepts, homiletical style, and cadence before they can draw on them for future reference, and I was very much in that beginner phase.

High Holiday sermons are the Super Bowl of a rabbi's year. These are the few services when most of your congregation will be present and paying close attention to your words, seeking their annual dose of inspiration. For a new rabbi, these sermons can sometimes make or break you. It was a high anxiety time for me because I was about to speak in front of thousands of extremely educated, experienced people who would see right through me if I wasn't duly prepared with a well-researched,

sufficiently thought-out expression. At Rodeph Sholom, our congregants were publishers, CEOs, television presidents, and other
professionals at the very top of their fields. They knew what was
intellectually honest and what was not. They didn't want information that they already knew—they wanted to hear something
innovative about what Jewish tradition and wisdom could teach
them on the matters of the day.

I awoke that fateful morning with a definite case of writer's
block. I wanted to speak about spirituality on Rosh Hashanah.
What was spirituality? How do we access it? It was such a big,
lofty subject, and the possibilities were endless. I remember
thinking of how popular cars on the market had names like
Odyssey and Quest. Could I make a link between the cars we buy
and the visions we have for ourselves—the exciting journeys we
hope to take in our lives? Would that speak to my congregants, or
would they think it was a stretch? I was stuck.

My fiancé Lauren and I had recently moved in together, a
few months before our wedding. That morning, she left for work
in the financial district as usual, and I went downstairs to the
gym in our Upper West Side apartment building to run on the
treadmill and clear my head before sitting down to work. I can
remember going over lines from my draft and wracking my brain
for better ways to phrase things and more inspirational texts to
quote as the local news played on the screen in front of me. Cars?
Did I really want to start off my sermon talking about cars?

I was lost in my own insecurities and couldn't get myself out
of the way. The way my own small problems seemed to loom over
me that morning as though they were supremely important will
always stay with me. I had no way of knowing that mere moments

later, reality as I understood it would shift profoundly, and these worries would soon be the furthest thing from my mind.

I was deep in my own thoughts and working myself into a healthy sweat on the treadmill, when I noticed something odd on the TV. There was smoke coming out of a building. The weather reporter was on, and she didn't seem to know what was happening, but the building was one of the Twin Towers. I remembered my father telling me that many years ago, in the 1940s, a plane had become disoriented in the fog and accidentally flown into a newly built skyscraper. I was alone in the basement gym and so preoccupied with my sermon that I didn't think much about this scene until I went back upstairs to get ready for the workday.

When I came into the apartment, the phone rang. It was Lauren, sounding panicked. Something was very wrong downtown. I turned on our TV, and the pieces began to fall into place. This wasn't an accident, that wasn't a small plane, and there was no fog in the bright blue sky. I remember asking her to turn around and start walking north. "Just come home," I pleaded. I wouldn't hear from her again for the rest of the day.

All the things that happened in the following hours will be forever imprinted on my spirit. At once sudden and unbearably elongated, the reality of the attacks came into focus for the world to see in real time—the planes crashing into the buildings, the billowing fires, the emergency calls to family members, the scenes of people fleeing the scene just in time, the images of others jumping out of windows to escape a fiery death inside the buildings, and finally, the horrific collapse of first one and then the other tower.

I was three months away from getting married, and I didn't know where my wife-to-be was, or if she was safe. I can still remember the phone ringing and one of the cantors from our synagogue calling to tell me that the first tower had fallen, suggesting we meet at our Jewish day school to organize ourselves for what was inevitably coming. Every detail of those hours is as clear to me today as it was in those moments over twenty years ago. I can hear the click of my flip phone snapping into my belt clip as I hurriedly grabbed my keys and ran out the door. I can feel the incongruous sunshine in my eyes as I ran outside, my heartbeat slamming in my chest as though I had never left the treadmill. I prayed that Lauren was safely making the long journey from Wall Street to the Upper West Side on foot, as I'd suggested. Our whole future was in the balance, and yet I had no choice but to spring into action and put thoughts of my own personal worst-case scenarios aside.

When we arrived at the school, everyone was in a state of shock and panic. Cell phones were primitive back then and networks were overloaded. It was impossible to get through to anyone. We were milling around and trying to come up with a feasible plan while silently praying for the thousands of people who we knew would be touched by the tragedy. We looked up every person we knew who worked in the towers and made a plan to walk to their homes and check on their families. We talked to the kids in school and tried to figure out how to tell them what had happened without causing them more stress than was absolutely necessary. We knew we needed to address things directly and that the way we responded on this day would be important for weeks and months, maybe even years to come.

All the while, stories of individuals started to pour in. It was already too much to bear. I remember knocking on a congregant's door on 76th Street. Andy worked in the World Trade Center. On the morning of September 11, many people were thankfully late to work because it was the first day of school in New York City and there was a primary election, so they were either taking their kids to school or voting before heading to the office. At least fifteen members of our synagogue avoided tragedy that day because of these events. Andy, however, had gone to the office as usual.

When he realized that a plane had hit his building, he called his wife Emily, who was home with their three young children. He described the nightmare of smoke and chaos that was happening in his office. He didn't know what exactly had happened, but he knew his situation was dire. He told her he loved her and the kids, and she recalls yelling into the phone, "Please, Andy, just get the hell out of there!" But before he could answer, the phone went dead. She would never hear his voice again.

When the door to their apartment opened, there were already at least ten other friends sitting with Emily as she waited to find out what had happened to Andy. The kids—a five, three, and one year old—were playing on the floor, unaware of what was happening or why their apartment was so crowded. Later that day, the one-year-old would take his very first steps, one of many milestones Andy would miss. His body was one of the first to be recovered and identified when rescue missions began.

Hours later, I walked back to my apartment in a daze. When I finally saw Lauren, around 4:00 p.m., she and I hugged in disbelief. She had not walked home in the morning when we first spoke, but went into her office instead. There, they covered the windows with wet towels as if there might be a nuclear war coming. When the buildings started to fall, they didn't know if they would fall vertically or right over onto her nearby office building, and she absolutely considered the possibility that she might die right then and there. She so vividly described the black cloud that enveloped the streets outside of her office window. It was hell on earth. It was madness and everyone was in shock and disbelief as the details of the attack became clear. Eventually, with all the subways shut down and the city in crisis, she and her co-workers made their way home on foot.

Lauren was clearly traumatized. Full of ash and soot from head to toe, her clothes in tatters, she kept talking about how surreal it had been, how I couldn't understand what she'd been through because I had spent my whole day uptown. I've often wondered if I should have headed downtown when I realized what was happening. I'm not sure what I could have done to help in those chaotic, horrific hours, but the opportunity hadn't presented itself. The work we were doing was necessary and urgent, and would continue to keep my colleagues and me working at a frenetic pace for months.

That night, glued to the news and unable to sleep, our wedding invitations arrived. The juxtaposition of these beautiful, cheerful reminders of our happy event and the reality of the day we had just lived through was jarring. Obviously, my immediate future would be filled with mourning and trauma. Funeral after funeral and shiva after shiva would follow for weeks to come. But I also knew that in just a few months, I would be blessed to begin a new journey with my wife, and our own future family was ahead of us. We had to survive and find a way to make meaning out of this senseless tragedy.

That week, we held daily prayer services, which was not our norm. Every night, hundreds of people gathered together to pray and be in community. Posters of missing people covered the walls of virtually every building in the city. Candles and flowers and impromptu memorials for those who were presumed dead were always in sight. On Shabbat, one thousand-two hundred people showed up for services and a vigil. One of the fallen for whom we mourned was our synagogue's security guard, who was also a firefighter. He had served the neighborhood at the station right down the block from our Temple and worked for us in the evenings to make extra money to support his growing family. He was killed trying to rescue people trapped in the buildings. I can still see his kind face to this day. He is indeed etched in my memory.

Everywhere you turned there was another person who had lost a loved one, another colleague missing, another child missing her parent. There seemed to be little to do but be there for one another and try to comfort each other through grief.

Many people were understandably paralyzed after 9/11. The scale of loss was unthinkable, and it was difficult to function in a usual way. But as a member of the clergy, there was a clear and present sense of necessary action. People needed a place to come and pray, a place to somehow find comfort from the communal misery, and we did everything we could to make that happen. They needed help planning unexpected funerals, and we worked closely with funeral homes and cemeteries who were themselves overwhelmed by the unusual volume. We all needed a safe space to mourn and also to find hope, and so we organized a candle-laden memorial in the lobby.

For people like Emily, who had lost her life partner and the father of her children at such a young age, we came together as a community and supported her in various ways for a full year. For six months, people took turns delivering meals to the family, arranging childcare, and literally sleeping on her couch every night to get her through those early days. Emily, who was not herself Jewish but had committed to raising her children in the tradition of their father's family, met with me once a week for counselling and advice on how to integrate Judaism into their lives without his help.

It was a time of intensive action and physical and emotional labor for all of us. For several weeks, we barely slept, holding back-to-back funerals and making shiva calls as bodies were recovered. Andy's funeral was one of the most wrenching services I have ever officiated. In the chaos of all the burials, the hearse bringing his body to the cemetery went to the wrong location, as the driver suffered a stroke. We waited three hours in pouring rain before the casket was finally delivered and we could lay Andy to rest. Hundreds of people stood there, huddled under umbrellas with mud puddling at their feet as five-year-old Hannah stood by the casket and said, in her small, sweet voice, "Goodbye, Daddy."

And while we dealt with the immediate aftermath of this enormous loss, the usual, natural cycles of life continued. There were births and baby namings, bar and bat mitzvahs, weddings, and yes, more deaths unrelated to terror attacks. Ten other congregants would pass away of natural causes in the ten days after

September 11. Their families tended to delay calling and making arrangements because they didn't want to burden us. It was an awkward time to be in mourning for a private loss that wasn't related to the Twin Towers, and yet we knew that those families needed to process their own mourning just as urgently as anyone else, and so we found ourselves officiating at funerals every single day.

The communal nature of the tragedy was something new to my generation, something that reminded older people of their experiences during world wars. Many people had lost spouses, friends, and co-workers under the same circumstances, on the same day, while the rest of us had experienced the collective trauma of watching horrific events play out in our midst, in real time. Naturally, this event was something we all needed to process. Our new normal was to compare our experiences with one another—where we had been that day, how our world was changed by the attacks, and who we had lost, were all topics of conversation at any gathering.

Until 9/11, I had always thought of grief as an intensely personal, private, and often lonely experience. Grief can be isolating and devastating for the ones who are working through it, which is why so many who are bereaved find themselves in support groups in the early days of healing. Because of the nature of the tragedy, our city became one giant communal support group, a tremendous source of comfort and understanding during a catastrophic time. At the same time, there was no escaping the tragedy, no way to set aside the trauma to re-set or focus on other things, because the whole city was grieving together. It was simultaneously comforting and suffocating.

There were many foundational lessons I learned about being a rabbi that year, but perhaps the most essential was to honor the ever-changing, day-to-day needs of congregants—sometimes they needed counsel and comfort, and sometimes they needed space—during these unique circumstances. In many ways, those weeks and months would become a sort of template for me, a rabbinic outline for how to function in times of extreme personal and communal crisis. Never could I have imagined that anything would equal the trauma of this experience, and in some ways nothing can. But in the years to come, I would shepherd my community through the financial crisis of 2008, the Tree of Life Synagogue shooting in Pittsburgh, and the COVID-19 pandemic, among other stressful situations. Through all of those experiences, I would return to the memory of 9/11 and its raw aftermath for guidance.

This was the first time in my life as a rabbi that I experienced something so traumatic that it knocked me back to an almost primitive spiritual state. Nothing mattered but dealing with the trauma and finding ways to heal and move forward. Nothing was as important as finding some kind of stability and "new normal." People needed to know how to pick up the pieces and find meaning in their lives again—how to get out of bed and go to work and fight through the fear that something like this might happen again.

It felt as if we had all been stripped to our very core. No longer could I give a sermon about cars and journeys and lofty ideals. As Rosh Hashanah finally approached, exhausted both emotionally and physically, I realized I had never finished drafting my sermon. There wasn't time to focus on writing and worrying about what people would think of me or what impression I wanted to make on the congregation. We were going to have unprecedented attendance that year, and our people were desperate for consolation. It was time to throw away the notes and speak from my heart.

That day, I spoke about resilience. I leaned into the feeling that, from now on, we needed to live a life of renewed purpose; we needed to find meaningful ways to feed our souls in our new, post-traumatic reality. Honestly, it may have been the best sermon I'd given at that point in my young career.

Later in the day, I walked to the water's edge with some congregants for the *tashlich* service, a ritual where one symbolically throws one's sins (in the form of pieces of bread) into a body of water to cast them away, hoping for a clean slate between Rosh Hashanah and Yom Kippur, the day of repentance that follows ten days later. As we walked along, the city air still pungent with smoke and ash, we saw members of the NY Rangers visiting local firehouses. This kind of unexpected sight was becoming more common as the city pulled together and celebrities did what they could to raise morale and help support the people who had lost coworkers and friends, not to mention their sense of safety and security in their home city. As we approached the Hudson River, one of my older congregants put his arm around me and said, "Son, today you became a rabbi." My eyes welling with tears, I knew he was right.

I've tried to recreate that Rosh Hashanah sermon many times over the years, and while I've never been able to remember it in detail, the message it taught has stayed with me. I would never again prepare a lofty, philosophical sermon with no basis in concrete reality. My goal was now to reach people where they were, to speak to their real-life experiences and concerns. That year, it was about reminding people of all the new reasons they had to live, to make the year to come a year of distinct purpose.

Ten days later, my Yom Kippur sermon was about the prayer *Unetane Tokef*, in which we acknowledge that we never know "who will live, and who will die," but that ultimately repentance, prayer, and charity are our best chances to help ourselves live a full, healthy life. This was our new reality. We were more vulnerable than we'd ever been, and the realization that we could no longer take our safety and security for granted was terribly burdensome. But we also knew that our only choice was to pick ourselves up, take responsibility for our lives, pray for our future, and help one another. It was a call to action unlike any of us had ever known.

The stench of fire and death was something we breathed in for months. Lauren couldn't sleep through the night for weeks after 9/11, and when she did, she would find herself breaking out in sweats and thrashing about with nightmares. I couldn't bring myself to go downtown for two whole months, until we needed to retrieve our marriage license. Witnessing the scene of devastation in person took my breath away. This was something we were going to live with forever. In many ways, our post-traumatic stress has still not dissipated completely.

But equally as palpable is the memory of how we responded to each other in a time of ultimate trouble. Police officers, fire fighters, emergency responders acted with a valor that redefined for us the meaning of heroism. We will never be able to repay what they did for us and our country that day. They will always be owed our deepest debt of gratitude. But everyday New Yorkers also acted in ways that kept us together. It didn't matter what one person believed about politics or for whom they had voted. Every person tried to help their neighbor. We held crying strangers in our arms, invited wandering people in for water and food, and we shared our stories. Most of all, we expressed our utter resolve to band together as New Yorkers and Americans to make sure that whatever had hit us would never be able to do so again.

Tragedy tends to bind people together, but this was more than a temporary commitment. It was built on a commitment of American comradery, of people seeing past their differences with a determination not to lose what we all felt so lucky to possess. Personally, I felt a renewed sense of patriotism and began to wear an American flag pin on my suit jacket for the first time in my life.

For a short while, it seemed that we were going to pull together as a nation and forgive our differences. But sadly, national healing was still elusive. American politics were always somewhat polarized, but after 9/11 things really shifted. I remember checking in with the Muslim owner of our neighborhood bodega, and it was clear that he was under extreme stress. People on high alert were already conflating Muslims with terrorists and business was not good. The road ahead would not be an easy one for him or his family.

One year later, I was making what would be one of my last house calls to visit Emily and her kids. They had come a long way over the course of the year. Hannah was now six, and the baby was a full-blown toddler, running through the apartment at top speed with toys in both hands. When the phone rang, Hannah reached for it and answered. We watched her pause and consider her words carefully. "No, I'm sorry," she said. "He's not here. And he's never coming back." She hung up the phone and Emily and I looked at one another. What was there to say? Hannah was right, and this was her reality. Our job was to be there for her as she grew up, to help her continue to come to terms with her father's death as she matured.

Hannah and her sister have both graduated from college at this point. Their brother will finish within a couple of years. We have never lost touch, and I have been at each of their major life events. Although I left Rodeph Sholom to lead my own congregation in 2006, I came back to attend their bat and bar mitzvah ceremonies as a joyful observer. They will always hold a special place in my life. All three kids have become incredibly successful young people, and I imagine they will do great and important things in this world. But whenever I look at them, I see an indelible sadness etched into their faces. Their lives will be good and meaningful, but their trajectories will always be defined by what happened on September 11. And so will mine and that of my rabbinate.

CHAPTER FIVE:

Living with Fear—Not in It

Hard on the heels of 9/11, we faced our next crisis—the anthrax scare of October 2001. Many of us were still struggling to perform basic tasks like going outside, riding the subway, or returning to office buildings without feeling a sense of panic. We were living in a constant state of existential angst and post-traumatic stress. Then news programs began reporting stories of a toxic powder in the mail, sent on purpose by a suspected terrorist. Just touching it would lead to significant health problems; breathing it in could kill you.

It truly seemed like the world was out of control and danger lurked around every corner. In those weeks and months after 9/11, everything seemed to change. We would soon be going to war with Afghanistan. Terrorism had infiltrated America in a way many people never expected to see in their lifetime. Security became tighter—not just at the airports, but in offices and certainly at synagogues. We had envelopes with white powder show up at our office, and at the offices of major Jewish Union organizations. People were afraid to go to the post office, and mail carriers were suddenly wearing surgical gloves and face masks. Our synagogue went from spending $100,000 a year on security guards, mainly for High Holiday services, to spending $500,000 and making sure we had armed guards at our doors at all times. Things were shifting, and not for the better.

I remember talking with my congregants about all these new, unfamiliar feelings. For the first time, many of them were realizing what it was not just to "have" a fear, but to be fully "inside" that fear. People truly didn't know how to process all of this anxiety without being paralyzed by it. A congregant told me that the one thing she was more scared of than flying was staying home. People began to leave the city in droves, often offering to pay a hundred thousand dollars over asking price for a home in the suburbs just to get away from Manhattan, which now felt dangerous in a whole new way. Many who stayed decided they would never ride the subway again and instead hired drivers or purchased cars. Some vowed they would never again fly in an airplane.

As Americans, the experience of having been attacked in our own home by a group of people who hated us was a new and terrifying reality with which we had no real experiential context. The closest I could remember to this kind of fear was the Iran Hostage Crisis in 1979, but even that was something happening thousands of miles away from our home front. My job, I knew, was going to be finding a way to help people as they navigated these unfamiliar waters and looked for a way to return to some kind of "new normal." Personally, I was more committed than ever before not only to New York City but to the country as a whole. I'd always felt a tremendous allegiance to Israel, but now I no longer took for granted the freedoms and liberties I had enjoyed as an American.

In many ways, the events around 9/11 helped American Jews who perhaps felt indifferent to Israel establish some kind of connection to the Jewish homeland. Having now been the victims of a crime of epic proportions—where suicide bombers sacrificed themselves as well as the lives of thousands of civilian victims and exhibited the kind of bottomless hate many could never have imagined possible—Americans began to empathize more with the people of Israel, who had been facing this kind of vengeful enemy for generations.

One year earlier, I had been planning my first-ever synagogue Israel trip. We had two full busloads of congregants signed up to travel with us and tour the Holy Land together, and I was beyond excited to share my love of the country with my community members. A few weeks before we were scheduled to leave, however, the Second Intifada broke out in Jerusalem. Suicide bombings and other acts of gruesome terror became a daily occurrence there. From a distance, the prospect of traveling to Israel seemed far too dangerous, and the majority of people who had signed up for the trip cancelled. I certainly understood why people were afraid to go, but it was important to me that we show our support for Israel during that turbulent time, so we shifted gears and decided to make it a solidarity mission.

In the end, thirty people decided to come along, and our experiences in that week were truly life-altering. This was my first time leading a congregational trip to Israel—something rabbis do on a somewhat regular basis—and I was doing so during one of the more perilous times in Israeli history. Commuter buses filled with civilians were blown up at random, and people who went to their regular cafes wondered if they might die eating their nightly fill of hummus and pita. I was proud of my congregation for stepping up and filling a bus without much cajoling on my part, as very few tourists were travelling to Israel at that time. The planes were virtually empty, as were the hotels.

Before we left for Israel, we held a Shabbat service at home, and all the attendees came to receive a blessing for a safe trip. Amazingly, hundreds more came to show solidarity with our mission. As they all bid us farewell, with tears in their eyes, they put wads of cash into our hands, asking us to use it to bolster the Israeli economy, which was hurting badly from the loss of tourism. I literally traveled with $15,000 in cash given to me that night.

When we arrived, we were put into a bullet-proof bus to protect us from all the random shootings that were coming from Palestinian towns into Israel proper. The bus driver literally yelled at us daily to stay seated on the bus because of the one inch of glass that was not bullet-proof at the top of the windows.

We were thorough in our approach to the trip. We visited the areas and people who were impacted the most by violence. We met with politicians from all sides of the political spectrum, including Palestinian leaders. We were there to show support and also to stand behind a nation who was searching for peace in the midst of horrific violence. With each passing day of our mission, we became more emboldened, listening to every story and expressing our unwavering support. All of us on the mission connected in incredibly deep ways because of what we were experiencing together. We talked into the middle of each night and found a deeper part of ourselves by dint of our journey.

And we also made sure to support the economy as much as possible. We ate out for every meal, and we used the cash our congregants had given us to generously tip every waiter, busboy, and shop clerk—often double or triple the normal amount. These Israeli workers, who are known for their gruff exteriors, could not stop thanking us for being there. It was a strange feeling for us, who were only there to show love and support, to be thanked by people whose lives felt in danger every day from the onslaught of terror.

I have led nearly twenty subsequent trips to Israel since that first trip in 2000. Although most of them have not, thank God, carried the same degree of danger, that trip helped me set a paradigm for every future group. My congregational trips to Israel have never simply been an exercise in travel, but in exploring the deepest parts of our faith, identity and complicated understanding of our relationship with our homeland.

Now, reeling from 9/11 just one year later, we were internalizing a life lesson our Israeli brothers and sisters had lived with for decades—a lesson we first experienced on that earlier mission to Israel. When you are surrounded by people who hate you, people who want you to cease existing, you must learn to live and love and go on with your daily routine, or you let the hate win.

Israelis had suffered so many of these terror attacks, and until the Twin Towers fell, many American Jews had a hard time relating to those of us who proudly and enthusiastically traveled to Israel in good times and bad to show our support. Instead of cancelling trips to Israel when these things happened, we would go anyway and sit in cafes, and support the economy, and prove to ourselves that going on with "normal" life is a choice we are all able to make.

Now, having suffered an attack on our own soil, there was a renewed (and for some, a brand new) sense of empathy for a country under near-constant attack. I'm sure that some of the people who traveled with me on that solidarity mission were scared and worried about what might have happened while we were there. The possibility of violence was more present than usual during that trip. But at the same time, those people grew attached to Israel in a more visceral way than they may have in other, more peaceful times.

It meant so much to me to share my connection with Israel with these brave and bold congregants. From my early childhood memories of the Munich Massacre and the Yom Kippur War to my gap year on kibbutz before starting college, Israel had always been special to me, a place that felt deeply ingrained in my soul. Now, as a rabbi in a large American congregation, I began to see the country through another set of eyes. How would I help my congregants relate to Israel, not only during these short trips throughout the years but also at home in the times between travels?

My mission in those months and years after 9/11 was to bring the lessons we learned in Israel in 2000 to my congregants who were suffering from fear and anxiety in Manhattan. Around the time that the anthrax scare was on the news every day, we were reading the Torah portion of *Lech Lecha* at services. In this biblical story, God tells Abraham, the father of monotheism, to leave behind his family and everything that he knows and embark on a journey to a new place where he and his descendants will become a great nation. This is an incredibly important story in Jewish tradition because it teaches us that, in order to affect great change, we have to make significant sacrifices, and we often have to leave behind everything that is familiar about our day-to-day lives.

The congregants who came with me on that trip to Israel were embodying the very heart of this biblical story. They journeyed far out of their home territory, at a time when things were full of risk and potential trauma, in order to fulfill a higher purpose. Until the anthrax scare, we had been slowly acclimating to our shared trauma of 9/11. Now, we were fully immersed in the experience of fear, knowing that the possibility of being a victim was as close as our mailboxes. We would have to do a great deal of inner work to steel ourselves for what lay ahead. Our world was forever changed, and it was up to us to choose whether we would remain stagnant in our current state of worry and panic, or if we would pick ourselves up and journey to a new place in our mental landscape.

CHAPTER SIX:

A Path of Growth

The years that followed 9/11 were a time of evolution and maturation in both my personal and professional life. Having faced the enormity of that day and its aftermath, the effects it had on individuals and our community as a whole, and experiencing my part in helping our community heal and move forward, I was more certain than ever that being a rabbi was indeed my calling. This was never going to be just a "day job" that I could leave behind at 5:00 p.m. And that was fine with me. In the same way that I knew I could never again give a sermon that wasn't based in authentic, contemporary experience, I knew that I wanted to focus on the bigger picture and help others do the same.

For a long time, I had avoided serious relationships and the idea of marriage. My childhood had been negatively impacted by my parents' divorce, and I wasn't sure I would ever want to risk such a relationship in my own life. In those early years of my rabbinate, I was careful to compartmentalize—to keep my personal and professional lives separate. This was necessary to protect my own privacy in those days, but the result was often that I needed to keep myself at an emotional distance from my congregation, careful not to let them into my life outside of the synagogue in order to maintain a healthy objectivity.

Now, later in life than many of my contemporaries, I was newly married and starting a family. Rodeph Sholom was my home, and I cherished my time there. My mother had once called it "the Harvard of synagogues," knowing that if I could succeed there, with the kind of high caliber, powerful members it attracted in Manhattan, I could succeed anywhere. Truly, just as I was conquering my personal fears of intimacy and commitment, I grew into my own professionally. Once I was established in a healthy, committed marriage, I was able to let my guard down a bit and really open up to my congregants on a personal level. This was instrumental in my professional development, because being a rabbi of a synagogue can be as much about participating in community events as it is about leading them, and I finally felt that I could let myself fully experience these events with my new family by my side.

It was during these years that I became interested in exploring Jewish spirituality more broadly. Many Reform synagogues were historically "classical"—meaning they were intellectual in their approach to Judaism, rather than emotional and spiritual. This worked for generations, but something was shifting in America, and I became fascinated by the interplay between Judaism and meditation, Buddhism, and experiential spirituality. I was accepted into a program at IJS, the Institute for Jewish

Spirituality. This was a new organization that focused on helping clergy explore their own spiritual lives so that we could bring back the same to our congregations.

Rabbinic seminary had provided us with excellent education and training, but many of us felt we still needed help to understand our own spiritual lives. IJS did exactly that. It pushed us to sit in silence, to find our inner wisdom, to understand the relationship between surface life and the ethereal. We studied and meditated. We slowed down our eating, exercising, praying, and studying so that we could see every subtlety in the ways we lived life. I was always a person who couldn't sit still, and so this work was hard for me. It brought out my insecurities and the disguises I wore to hide my most vulnerable sense of self. Now, I was learning to embrace the characteristics that challenged me and make them my strength.

It had always been important to me to be a rabbi who had a broad knowledge of Jewish practice and who could lead services not just in my own Reform congregation, but in any synagogue of any denomination. I wanted to be a rabbi who sparked a deeper spiritual experience for people, rather than one who gave them a performance to watch. By doing so in my own life, I was able to share appropriately that same sense of vulnerability with my congregation. I grew and thus, I think, so did they.

As I deepened my own knowledge and experience, I began to think about what was next in my career. I had started out at Rodeph Sholom as a rabbinic intern and was hired just after I was ordained. It had been a richly rewarding experience, and it was entirely possible for me to stay on as an assistant rabbi for many more years to come. But to do that would mean that I would not have the opportunity to advance my rabbinate, to learn what it meant to truly lead a congregation and help to shape the course of its future. This was not the end of the world, but I was finally feeling like I was ready to venture out on my own, and so I began to keep my eyes open for new opportunities.

Fairly soon after I began interviewing, I was offered the position to lead a smaller synagogue in the city. The place needed a huge amount of work to build up membership and create a thriving community. As I considered this move, one of my most respected mentors advised me that it was a great opportunity, but if I took it, I should expect to do nothing but eat, sleep, and breathe that synagogue for the next five years. I looked at Lauren and our small, growing family, and I knew that I couldn't afford to give up those years of their early childhoods. I'd waited so long to start my family, I wanted to enjoy them and be fully present as they grew up. I still worried about my ability to sustain a marriage given my childhood and so I knew I had to give myself the best shot at understanding what it meant to be a husband and eventually a father. And so, I turned down that job, knowing something else would come up.

It soon became obvious that the only way I was going to get into an established synagogue as a senior rabbi was to leave New York City. I hadn't yet served enough years to be qualified to lead a mega-sized Temple in the City. In any case, there were no such openings available. Lauren was in no rush to leave the city, and I honestly had a hard time imagining us living anywhere else. I remember talking about this quandary with one of my colleagues, who told me, "Listen, if you need to take a fourth quarter shot, go and find your own place to run." I'd loved my years at

Rodeph Sholom, but I didn't want to look back with any degree of resentment, and that was going to happen if I were to stay there for much longer. We were going to have to make some big decisions, and soon.

In the fall of 2005, I received a call about an opening to be the senior rabbi of B'nai Jeshurun, a Reform congregation in Short Hills, NJ. Eighteen miles from Manhattan, Short Hills is an affluent suburb where many residents commute to the city for white collar jobs on Wall Street. The synagogue had a storied history. Founded in 1848 by a band of German immigrants, it began in Newark and eventually moved to Short Hills in 1968. To lead one of the largest synagogues in the state with close to five thousand members and a budget of $9 million a year was no small job, especially for a fairly junior rabbi. We knew it was a long shot, but it seemed like a good idea to go and check it out.

This synagogue was in transition. Their previous senior rabbi had retired after fifty years of service. As a community that did not love change, they had assumed that the junior rabbi, who had spent fifteen years under the former rabbi's tutelage, would step into the role seamlessly. However, after just three years on the job, he came to the realization that he simply did not want to act as the CEO of the synagogue in addition to his significant pastoral role. For better or worse, B'nai Jeshurun needed someone who could both pastor *and* run the business end of things. So they were now in the position of looking for an outside hire.

At least thirty-five other rabbis were vying for the position, including some rather experienced big shots. I was realistic about my slim chances as I pulled up to the elaborate driveway, shaking my head at the absurdity of the whole thing. I had visited this synagogue once before to attend a wedding (in true "small world" fashion, the bride was a fellow rabbinical school student, and her father was the senior rabbi of B'nai Jeshurun). I can remember being in awe of the giant parking lot with room for thousands of cars and the imposing structure of the building itself, by far the tallest in Short Hills. I never could have imagined then that I would be considered for a job like this, nor that I would even have considered applying for it. But here we were.

Ten minutes into the interview, much to my own dismay, I'd fallen in love. Nothing could have prepared me for how quickly I connected with the members of the search committee and how at home I felt there. The scene was not made for love at first sight. As part of my application, I'd already submitted a vision statement detailing how I planned to direct the Temple, with sample sermons, lesson plans for the religious school and adult education classes, and more. Now, I walked into a board room to face some thirty members of the congregation, representing many different demographics. While one member interviewed me, any other member was free to ask follow-up questions on topics as wide-ranging as my views on God, ethics, membership, fundraising, relationships with children, angry congregants, or officiating at interfaith and gay marriages. My counseling abilities were tested when I was asked rhetorical questions about how I would deal with sudden tragedy. They also grilled me about my views on politics in both America and Israel. The sheer pace and scope of these conversations should have been utterly overwhelming. Instead, it was invigorating, even energizing and fun.

My senior rabbi and mentor had advised me to think about whether or not our souls connected during this initial meeting.

He told me that my interview should not be an intellectual exercise alone, but a spiritual one as well. I needed to find out if we had the potential to be covenantal soul mates.

What Rabbi Levine meant was that this wasn't a moment to figure out if I wanted to move from New York City to Short Hills, but to know if we were a match spiritually. Did our values align? Did we care about people in the same ways? Would we be able to overcome conflict when it inevitably arose? Did they have a good sense of humor and understand when to take life seriously and when not to? Did we connect the way a couple would naturally connect on a great date?

The relationship between a rabbi and a congregation really is like a marriage. Our lives are inextricably connected. Rabbis are there for the most pivotal moments in a congregant's life, from birth through various life cycle events, illnesses, and death. It is a sacred relationship, and when it stops working or ends for any reason, it can be as painful and traumatic as a divorce.

Until my interview at B'nai Jeshurun, I hadn't experienced this level of connection. Our souls seemed in tune on deeply important issues, and our conversations felt both familiar and familial. It was an unexpected and easy bond between a young, urban rabbi and an established, older suburban congregation, but somehow it just felt right.

The next day they called and made it obvious that they were just as pleasantly surprised as I had been. Two months later, I was offered the position.

Lauren and I struggled with the idea of leaving our life in the city and all of our friends. It wasn't the congregation itself that made me hesitant, but the idea of moving out of my comfortable liberal bubble. I had grown up in Manhattan, and leaving the Upper West Side meant I would no longer enjoy the comfort of being surrounded by my own left-leaning politics and what I saw as its connection with Jewish practice. I prejudged the suburbs as a place of political apathy, filled with people who wanted to be as far out of the fray as possible in terms of balancing the scales of justice in the world. New York City didn't just represent action for me; it was a place of sophistication and intellectual where-withal. But in the end, we decided to embrace the opportunity to grow and develop my rabbinate and to try out life in the suburbs.

My first Shabbat at B'nai Jeshurun coincided with the Fourth of July weekend in 2006. Normally, this is not a well-attended service, since so many families are out of town for the holiday. But this year, many families stayed to come check out this new "Rabbi Matt." The previous week, fifty people came to services. That day, despite the national holiday, three hundred people were in attendance.

People were excited about the change in leadership, but they didn't quite know what to expect. Many Reform synagogues held on to their staunchly classical mode for decades, and TBJ was no exception. Until the 1940s, they maintained an anti-Zionist platform, arguing that Jewish attachment to Israel meant opposition to American values. Everything was black and white; there was no nuance to balancing a love for Israel and living as a proud American Jew. No one wore kippot or tallitot when I arrived. And "Rabbi Matt"? They were used to a far more formal relationship with their leaders.

I had never been comfortable with classical Reform practice. Ironically, I felt that those practices were more "orthodox" than Orthodoxy itself. People think of traditional Orthodoxy as a strict adherence to codes of dress and conduct. But in my mind, classical Reform practices were just as restrictive—they were orthodox in their opposition to anything outwardly Orthodox.

I knew immediately that there were things I wanted to change and that I was committed to being the rabbi I wanted to be. I knew that they were likely worried about all these changes and how they would be affected by them, even if they weren't sure why the idea disturbed them.

My hope was to approach change as an evolution rather than a revolution—to grow with the congregation and win them over with time and shared experience. We had a long road ahead of us. Change would be difficult, as it always was, but it was also necessary to help rejuvenate the synagogue and keep it thriving into the future. The president of the Temple urged me to act as a rudder, balancing innovation with tradition and respect for the congregation's history. My first task was to get to know the people I now led, their stories and their generations of connection to the synagogue. Ours is an institution that has significance not just for individual families but for the community at large. I wanted to honor the historical value of the Temple—both personal and communal—while helping it evolve into a place where members could find an authentic, fulfilling connection to God. But in order to reach my loftiest goals, I would need to start small and become a member of the community myself.

My first task was to give a sermon at that Fourth of July Shabbat service. Sermons don't necessarily make or break a rabbi but certain sermons can go a long way in either direction. A rabbi's first sermon at a congregation is his or her first impression. Members are often eager to see what the new rabbi has to say, what kind of presence they bring to the table.

That first Shabbat, I talked about optimism and hope. My son often jokes with me that all I ever talk about from the pulpit is hope. Perhaps he is correct. There are many virtues that I hold up as superlative, but none is more important to me than the chance for a better tomorrow. This community had been stagnant for a while. They were taking a chance on me and my relative youth and inexperience. I was taking a chance on a community that was very different from the liberal urban cocoon of Rodeph Sholom. We were all wading into the unknown, but also into an opportunity to chart a new course, replete with excitement and, yes, hope. I knew I couldn't come in like a bull in a china shop. I made them understand that I had studied their grand history carefully and would do my best to build upon it so that we could become the leading light of synagogues in the state. From the beginning, I did my best to be open and honest, vulnerable and loving.

Because we had expected a fraction of the crowd that showed up, my first service was held in the smaller chapel rather than the one thousand-two hundred-seat main sanctuary. As a result, the room was packed, and I remember being worried that our two-year-old son, Jake, might try to run up to me on the pulpit, as he was used to doing at Rodeph Sholom. I had been warned that this would look far too informal and that the regulars would not be pleased with such a display.

I got up on the bima to give my sermon and took a deep breath. We were at the start of our journey together, so I spoke of the biblical story of the twelve spies who were sent into the land of Israel to bring back intel on the Promised Land. Ten spies came back with tales of fear and trepidation, sure that entering the land would lead to certain defeat. But Caleb and Joshua talked of a land of milk and honey, optimistically sure that the wandering Hebrews could conquer the land and secure it for themselves.

As with every new venture, I said, one could focus on the difficulties ahead, or the promise and beauty. I was sure that we could be like Caleb and Joshua, taking our first steps into the unknown together with our eyes and hearts open to possibility. The resounding, enthusiastic "Amen!" I heard from those hundreds of congregants was something I will always remember.

And then, just as we were singing the closing song, the maintenance man (himself an incredibly respected staple of the synagogue for thirty years) walked in holding my son's hand, and Jake impulsively ran to me with his sweet and inviting smile. To my delight, the congregants didn't gasp in horror, but instead there were adoring chuckles and quite a few teary eyes. It was then that I knew that while we still had much to learn, we had truly found a new home in the suburbs.

* * *

That first summer, I did my best to connect with as many current members as possible, visiting homes for about thirty "meet the rabbi" coffees. We would drink coffee and eat snacks, learn a little Torah, touch on current events, and get to know one another. The members who came to these coffees told me about their lives and their connections to the Temple, and what they thought the community needed to thrive once again. They asked me about my stance on ritual, political, or communal policies. They told me what made them feel close and what pushed them away, eager to be known and cared for on a personal level and anxious to connect with Judaism on a deeper level.

One of the common themes I heard was that the Temple had stopped speaking to the times at hand. They wanted leadership to respond to what was happening in the world. For example, they wanted to know what I planned to do about same sex marriage and intermarriage. When I told them about my experience at Rodeph Sholom, when I took six months to study and reflect with my congregation before committing to perform same sex weddings, they seemed pleased. They appreciated that I planned to take some time to get to know them and to weigh the various sides of the thorny intermarriage debate before establishing a policy.

By the time my first high holiday season came up, I'd already made personal connections with four hundred of the eight hundred families in our membership roster. In those early months, I also did a little "surface" work—changing the way our office staff answered the phones, updating our logo and stationery—to make the place more professional, modern, and most of all, warm and welcoming. With a healthy shuffle of staff and some dynamic new hires, we began to think about how to market the synagogue to those who felt disenfranchised from Judaism. I wanted B'nai Jeshurun to be a thriving intellectual and spiritually fulfilling center for all those who chose to join us.

To do that I made sure we had an exciting lineup of guest speakers and adult education classes on various topics. I brought politicians like Senator Cory Booker and then-U.S. Attorney (and future governor) Chris Christie to speak, as well as great journalistic minds like David Brooks and Tim Russert. We spent time with writers like Bob Woodward, Mitch Albom, and Tom Friedman, who shared their expertise about politics and writing but also their own spiritual journeys and how their inner lives affected their respective lines of work. I was trying to make our sacred home a "brave space," one where we could openly learn and talk about all disciplines and then try to connect and see them through a Jewish and spiritual lens. I wanted my congregants to know they didn't have to go to Manhattan to find stirring intellectual and spiritual inspiration. It was now regularly going to be found right here in Short Hills, New Jersey.

The excitement around these events was extraordinary. We had between five hundred and two thousand attendees each time, and people were thrilled to have these new and different opportunities to gather together, learn, and socialize outside of religious services. Meaning and wisdom and relevance were right there for the taking.

At the same time that we were reaching out to the future, I wanted to reconnect with the synagogue's original urban roots in Newark. Together with the Episcopal bishop of Newark and the most prominent Imam from the area, we created what we called the Newark Interfaith Coalition for Hope and Peace. Our mission was to combat gang violence in the area by creating a safe space focused on what we had in common rather than what separated us as different communities. I would take members to Newark and walk the streets during festivals, connecting with the neighborhood. I even had members of the infamous Bloods and Crips come to our synagogue to talk about violence and poverty, reconciliation, and paths for peace.

For members young and old, it was exciting—and very different from what they were used to. Everything was on the table. If it was compelling and potentially life-altering, I thought it was worth trying. We all felt that we were changing the narrative and trajectory of the community and at the same time rekindling a long and storied congregation that was taking its rightful place as a leader amongst synagogues nationally. In retrospect, it was my youthful exuberance that enabled me to be so bold. I probably would have been far more cautious had I known then what I understand now about congregational politics, since one wrong move would have really cost me valuable "capital" with the community. Luckily, it all went well, and our membership was inspired and ignited by the new and fresh energy.

As all of this was happening, I was also writing my first book, which had been bought by a publisher just as I took the job and would be released a year later. The book was about grief and reflected my experiences of dealing with the myriad losses around the events of September 11, 2001. As I thought back to those events that defined my early rabbinate, I was so grateful to be starting out in suburban New Jersey at a time when nothing earth-shattering was happening.

I think people appreciated all the time and energy I was pouring into the community, and there began to be a buzz around town that B'nai Jeshurun was the place to be. More and more people started showing up to our events, and then to Shabbat services. Slowly but surely, they began to fill out membership applications and enroll their babies and toddlers in nursery school and their older kids in Hebrew school. After eighteen months, we were up to about one thousand one hundred families, and more people were coming to check us out week after week. Things could not have been going better for me as a new senior rabbi and for this community who had been looking to turn a new leaf, and these were some of the more formative years of my life and rabbinate. I was a New York City native who had belittled New Jersey my whole life, yet here I was enamored of this new community which had become my home so quickly.

CHAPTER SEVEN:

Stepping Out on My Own

New Jersey is a blue state, but while its people are for the most part socially liberal, they also tend to be fiscally conservative. Republican governors Tom Kean, Christine Todd Whitman, and Chris Christie were all handily elected in this Democratic stronghold. As I got to know my new congregants, I discovered many who believed in smaller government and fewer taxes. They had less trust in the government than my former liberal congregants and worried that corruption in governmental programs could bring down decent and hardworking people. They had nimbly voted for candidates from both parties while advocating for their beliefs.

I encountered less interest in social engagement than I was used to in Manhattan, where political activism was occurring on every corner. I didn't find the constant hunger to talk politics and political advocacy. Still, my new community was, and still is, steadfastly devoted to making our world a more just place, but their way of balancing the scales of justice did not always follow the path that I, and perhaps many in the Reform Movement, were used to.

It didn't take long for me to realize that many of my congregants had an intrinsic prejudice towards me. They initially expected that I was automatically in the tank with the Democratic Party and had pledged allegiance to the party's positions, literally passing some partisan litmus test in order to be ordained as a Reform rabbi. They asked if I could love and faithfully pastor to them since they were Republicans. They wondered if I would attempt to inculcate liberal values into their children in religious school. I initially found their assertions nonsensical and wondered if moving to the suburbs had been a horrible mistake .

One member in particular posed a challenge. He and I had had some spirited debate over the issue of the Tea Party. To put it mildly, we were on opposing sides of that issue. For me, these political conversations were separate from my pastoral work with this member, but he was concerned that because of our differing politics, I might not give his child my full attention at his upcoming bar mitzvah. The assertion was hurtful and offensive to me, but I also understood his concern. In some way, I must have contributed to his perception of me. Many other members had made passing comments about my "bleeding heart," and I was able to dismiss most of them as insignificant, if uncomfortable. But in this case, I felt I needed to address the misperception head on. I might disagree with a person's politics, but my first priority would always be to pastor them fairly and with a full heart, "bleeding" or otherwise.

When the day of this family's bar mitzvah came, I could sense the relief mixed in with the usual emotions of joy and celebration. My liberal politics had not affected my ability to officiate the service or give their son a meaningful, heartfelt charge after he read from the Torah and gave his speech.

Ultimately, in those early days, most members simply wanted me to give relevant sermons and to keep an open mind. They were bored by sterile oratory. They wanted to be made to think more, to challenge their assumptions about the world. And so I did. I asked, from my sermons that they look to subtleties, to struggle with nuance. I pushed them to remove themselves from their own echo chambers to hear what the other side had to say. I encouraged a civility of purpose and bravery. I suggested that we stand up for our values but to not be so sure that we owned the truth. Not only might others within our circles have something to teach us, but perhaps, even those to whom we are diametrically opposed could educate us as well.

Even so, without realizing it, I was still preaching that the path to social justice was through a politically liberal understanding of the world. The congregants were no longer bored by the sermons, but they did wonder out loud if I might "tone it down" a bit. Congregants would often call, write, or schedule in-person meetings to let me know how my frank and strongly-worded sermons had made them feel—and those feelings were not always positive.

I laughed in righteous indignation, thinking they only wanted to be compelled to action if the philosophy behind it was their own. This was a new relationship, and it seemed we both needed to grow together to understand what we all intended. My sermons were not replete with political vitriol, but there were absolutely some layers of unconscious political bias, and I imagine that from their point of view, their own biases colored how they reacted to mine.

Instead of reacting hastily, I decided to look in the mirror and think deeply about my own assumptions. Were they concerned about my politics, or were they worried that because my politics didn't align with theirs, I might not be there for them pastorally? I was compelled to explore this question because I saw that this community did extraordinary amounts of work to help surrounding communities become whole. They were the first to open a homeless shelter in our county; one of the first in the region to start a weekly food pantry; and their bins of donated food, clothing, diapers, and the like were always overflowing. Many of the members of my new congregation were more instinctively conservative than my upbringing, but my reaction to that conservatism was based on my previous experiences and not about their actual concrete commitment to fixing our broken world. It would take years for me to undo my instinct to conflate liberal and Jewish values and open myself up to other, equally valid expressions of political and religious engagement, but this was a start.

My evolution as a human being and as a rabbi took a turn during those early years at B'nai Jeshurun. I found my training at Rodeph Sholom had absolutely prepared me to lead my own Temple. I became a more confident preacher, leader, and teacher. I woke up every day with new and creative ideas for how to reach further and deeper into my congregation. I was becoming more expedient. Words flowed more easily and my pastoral instincts grew exponentially. I learned what it meant not to just lead a sacred community spiritually, but how to ensure that our Temple ran smoothly and solvently.

Despite the intensity of it all, the honeymoon period in New Jersey was extraordinary. I literally felt the excitement of being a rabbi every day and challenged myself and my leadership to grow in every facet of congregational life. I wanted the lights to be on every night, so the building could be an epicenter for communal life. I worked fourteen hours a day in those early years, and I couldn't get enough. My life was my family and my congregation, and it was utterly fulfilling. This process of creating a relationship with my new congregation made me listen more deeply and carefully than I had before.

Perhaps because my rabbinic and mental bandwidth was wider than it had been when I was younger, I was able to listen to all parts of what my congregants were revealing to me without feeling defensive. I started to understand shades of difference myself, and I opened to the possibility that perhaps they had something to teach me too.

For the first time, these "others" were a part of my spiritual and social life. Our congregation was a warm and welcoming place, and the members truly wanted to include me in their conversations. They sent me articles to read and stopped by to chat, respectfully curious about my take on current events and eager to share their own perspectives. Over coffee and cake after services, at a monthly bike ride I took with a group of TBJ men, and around town after hours, I found myself in conversation with so many new and interesting people. I didn't turn towards conservatism, necessarily, but I made a commitment to hear better and listen more deeply. When I heard other points of view being expressed, I did my best to consider them as valid and valuable, rather than immediately discounting them with biblical texts and rabbinic voice. I was not going to make any headway with this group of people if I spent all of my energy trying to get them to "see the light" as I saw it.

At first, I feared I was betraying myself, my upbringing, and my rabbinic training just by allowing myself to be open. But I soon realized I had been betraying myself by not sincerely and authentically listening to their arguments and philosophies. And so, I used these social gatherings as opportunities to listen to differing points of view on fiscal policy, immigration, second amendment rights—anything and everything that was percolating in the news.

When I attended study groups or rabbinical conferences throughout the country, some of my colleagues said that my job was explicitly to counsel my congregants to the "blue," "left," enlightened way of thinking. They thought it was my duty to preach against the war in Iraq and rail against border security. Many of them were reflexively responding without leaving open the possibility that there were other legitimate opinions to mitigate the same societal issues about which they and we always worried. I believe in equal rights, compassion for all people, and racial equality. I believe in ending hunger and homelessness and the establishment of a Palestinian State. But I learned that my job wasn't to get my congregants to vote differently; it was to persuade them to advocate for justice, no matter which path they took to that end.

* * *

During these honeymoon years, despite a few inevitable bumps along the way, it was smooth sailing.

We had welcomed two hundred new families into our congregation rather quickly, and things were growing and changing every day. Meanwhile, some of the members who had left began to filter back. They thought this was a moment to give their synagogue a second chance. Along with returning members came people who had heard the buzz and wanted to see what all the renewed energy was about.

However, before I knew it, we were faced with a series of crises beyond the scope of normal, and our honeymoon came to abrupt halt. Now it was time to see if the newly energized community could sustain itself in the face of tragedy and upheaval.

In 2008, I was writing my sermon for Rosh Hashanah. This year, I was hard at work on a very personal, transformative sermon reflecting my shifting position on interfaith marriage. Every year, I aim to make my high holiday sermons a sort of spiritual challenge for the year ahead, tackling the big issues of the day and grappling with difficult subjects that will affect our lives going forward. Intermarriage is a huge topic for any rabbi, and for me it had tremendous personal significance. All three of my siblings had married outside the faith, and all had asked me to officiate at their weddings. I had said no every time, as this was not a position I was ready to take in those days. Many would surmise that officiating at gay and interfaith marriages occupied the same place on the rabbinical spectrum. But in my mind, it was much clearer for me to take the path of officiating at gay marriages as long as both partners were Jewish. I had stood firm in my stance against intermarriage for years, and it had been a source of pain and conflict within my own family.

But in the last few years, I had been doing more research, both theological and sociological, and came to the conclusion that I would have to change my philosophy in order to meet the changing needs of the Jewish community. I had come to believe that we would have a better shot at sustaining the Jewish community by welcoming interfaith families into the community rather than turning them away.

Rodeph Sholom had forbidden officiation of interfaith marriage, and up to that point, no cleric had ever officiated at such a marriage at B'nai Jeshurun. It was an issue utterly fraught with complicated feelings. Both sides cared passionately about the survival of Judaism, and both argued that to go one way or the other would bring about the demise of the Jewish community. Either you sanctioned the watering-down of the religion by allowing couples to intermarry, or you risked alienating the Jewish spouses altogether by rejecting them. I planned to announce that I would now officiate at weddings for mixed-faith couples who agreed to raise their children as Jews; to me, this compromise seemed the best solution to a complicated problem.

One night, as I was working on this sermon in my home office, Lauren came in abruptly and blurted out, "Lehman Brothers is shutting down. It is about to go belly up!"

I didn't quite register what she meant. Lehman Brothers was a huge investment banking firm. They didn't "close." I told her I was busy writing my sermon on intermarriage. She firmly told me that I would have to wait on that one for another year. The financial world was about to implode, and as I well knew, our community was filled with financial advisors and bankers and investors who worked in Manhattan. They were not going to care much about my new openness to interfaith marriage when their whole world was collapsing around them and their future financial stability was at risk.

Lauren is one of those spouses who is loving enough to tell me what I need to hear, even when that truth is uncomfortable. She implored me to open my eyes because the world was about to fall apart; a run on the banks was not a remote possibility and a severe recession was not just possible, but probable.

My heart sank. I knew the world was about to change in ways that I had only heard about from my father, who grew up during the Depression. I had no idea what to expect, but it was obvious that I had to change gears, and fast.

Sure enough, on Rosh Hashanah, the market dropped 777 points. People walked into services that night pale and shell-shocked. I had not seen such collective devastation since the events of 9/11. You could feel the tension, and the stress in the sanctuary was palpable. This was a room full of successful professionals. Until that moment, they had exuded confidence in every way. Suddenly, they were deflated and worried. They had supported me as I came into their lives to help revitalize their synagogue, and now it was time for me to support them, spiritually and emotionally, as they faced a really difficult situation.

That Rosh Hashanah, instead of intermarriage, I spoke about loss. What do we do when faced with the possibility of losing every material thing that we have? How do we live in relation to our money, and what does it mean to us at the end of the day, when we put our whole lives in perspective? I spoke about my own history—how after my parents divorced, we struggled financially, and as a teenager I found myself working to buy my own clothes and sometimes even food. My parents had two homes to maintain and four children to juggle, and sometimes it was a stretch for them to make ends meet. I spoke about Jewish ethics on money and how we were going to rally as a community to make sure our members were safe and sound as they navigated their new realities.

My congregation appreciated the honesty. Honesty was really all we had left. Most of the people who worked in Wall Street circles lost two thirds of their income. Many of them would never again make as much money as fast as they'd made it before. To their credit, they took me up on my offer to talk about what counted most in life. I gathered with many congregants both individually and collectively to talk through what it meant to create a life of meaning and purpose with less means. It was counterintuitively transcendent for the congregation. People dug into themselves and evaluated their lives in ways I had not experienced before, and I believe they found a depth from within that, though it would not refill their bank accounts, helped them discover a new source of intention and fulfillment in the world.

* * *

In the year that followed, we saw many families struggle as a result of the financial crisis. Some marriages ended and some managed to grow stronger as they faced these new hardships together. For the first time in its history, the wealthy community

of Short Hills, New Jersey, set up a foundation for helping people with their bills. My synagogue president and I had a serious
conversation about what we would do if people truly lost everything, facing homelessness, and how we needed to set up a temporary shelter in our space. There was a palpable fear that this
might end up being a moment in history as crushing as the Great
Depression.

This was, for me, a crash course in the business end of running a synagogue. We needed to make the tough decisions that
come with significant budget cuts. We had spent a few years
expanding our community, renovating the physical façade of the
building, and developing our spiritual and philosophical stances.
Now, there was a hiring freeze and no raises for staff for the foreseeable future. We had families who suddenly couldn't afford the
tuition for Hebrew school or who had to pull their young children out of our early childhood center to save money.

Sometimes, the life of a rabbi seems to revolve around one
tragedy after another. In the midst of the fallout from the financial crisis, our community faced two back-to-back personal crises that would affect me profoundly.

One day in late December 2008, when I was on my way to
join my family for a much-needed vacation in Connecticut, I
received a call from my assistant rabbi. He was trying to catch
his breath and get the words out as quickly as possible, clearly
in a panic. Cynthia Wayne, a nursery school teacher who was
beloved by the community for decades, had unexpectedly died
in front of her class full of young children. A healthy sixty-eight-
year-old woman with no known health conditions, Cynthia had
suddenly collapsed after clutching her chest. The toddlers who

witnessed this event were quickly ushered out of the room while her coworkers administered CPR and waited for the paramedics to arrive. Sadly, she was pronounced dead upon arrival at the hospital.

Any sudden death is painful and traumatic, but because she was so well known in the community, Cynthia's passing was especially difficult. Not only did her family suffer from her loss, but the levels of trauma experienced by her young students, their parents and siblings, and all the other teachers and staff in the school where she had worked for thirty years made her death a community-wide disruption. I had to turn around and head back to the Temple to help everyone cope with the shock and attend to funeral plans with the family.

A few days later, Rabbi Barry Greene, the former head of the Temple, who was supposed to co-officiate Cynthia's funeral, also died suddenly at the age of seventy-eight. Rabbi Greene had served the Temple for fifty years, and although we were very different in our approaches to Judaism, he had always been gracious and welcoming to me, obviously rooting for my success. Because we got along so well, and because he was so beloved among the congregants, I had been relieved when he offered to help officiate lifecycle ceremonies (usually funerals) of congregants of his own generation, with whom he had such deep connections. It is especially challenging to eulogize people you do not know well, and given his years of experience in the community he was literally irreplaceable.

On the morning of Cynthia's funeral, I woke up at 6:00 a.m. to polish my part of the eulogy, hoping to strike the right balance and help the family as much as possible as they began their mourning process. At 6:45, the phone rang. This is never a good sign. It was a former president of the Temple, a highly respected member of the community.

"Charlie? What is it?"

He got right to the point. "Matt, Barry Greene dropped dead of a heart attack just now. He never made it to the hospital. The EMTs couldn't revive him."

"What are you talking about?" I asked.

"Matt," he replied in an exacting tone, "this is the reality. We need you to pop into action."

I immediately called Barry's wife and daughters, one of whom was my close friend and rabbinical school classmate. I then had to inform my team, most of whom had known Barry for years. Then I had to figure out what I was going to say to Cynthia's family. Not only were they about to bury their mother, wife, and grandmother, but they would have to be told of their rabbi's sudden death on the day he was to help with her funeral. The ceremony was about to take place at 10:00 a.m. Much as I wanted to, I couldn't put off telling them the truth and make something up about Barry not being able to make it. They needed to know, even on this most difficult of days.

It is customary for a rabbi to meet with the family in a private room before the start of a funeral service for words of comfort and to review the details of the service. During that meeting, I told them what had just happened to Barry. Honestly, I was worried that the shock of this loss on top of the one they were already experiencing might be too much. I worried that Cynthia's husband might have a heart attack of his own on the spot. Of course, the news was incredibly upsetting and added another level of sadness to an already horrific day.

As soon as we entered the sanctuary filled with one thousand mourners who had come to pay their respects to Cynthia, I could tell that the news of Barry's sudden passing was making its way through the crowd. So many faces looked pale and drawn, and it almost seemed too much to bear. I knew that in a few days' time, many of these same people would return for Barry's funeral. Even today, many years later, it sends a chill down my spine to remember the emotions of those two tremendous losses, back-to-back. At the time, Lauren was pregnant with our third child, and for me, the juxtaposition of sudden death and impending birth was personally overwhelming. That week was the kind of clustered tragedy that would test the most experienced clergy. Here I was, just trying to get my feet wet, and suddenly I was splashing around in the deep water.

As a new rabbi of an established congregation, there are always some growing pains. One way to help ease the community into such a big transition is to build relationships with past leaders, like the ones I'd been building with Rabbi Greene. With both of them gone so suddenly, we were all reeling. Beyond the deep sadness I felt for their losses, I was also worried about how I would bridge the gap from their generation to my own without their guidance and approval.

* * *

The next fall, I was in my home office at midnight, feverishly writing and re-writing the sermon I would give three days later on Yom Kippur, when my phone rang. At that hour, the sound of a phone ringing can only mean tragedy and drama, which was the last thing I needed. Three thousand people would be paying close attention to my Yom Kippur sermon, evaluating my performance—and my politics. I knew they were still unsure about me, and I needed my sermon to be a grand slam. So I was agonizing over every word when the acoustical bomb of a ringing phone shattered the silence.

I reached for the phone and heard a distraught woman's voice. It took me a beat or two to recognize her—a woman I knew through a program she participated in at the temple. Something truly terrible had happened. Her son, a college student, was in a hospital in Philadelphia having suffered a spinal cord stroke, a condition rarely seen in young people.

"And," she said, choking back a sob, "if he lives, he's almost for sure going to be a quadriplegic."

My heart sank and my mind raced. To give myself time to organize my thoughts, I encouraged her to keep talking. It's a tendency I've had all my life, hesitating to express an opinion or judgment. It has, on balance, served me well, especially when negotiating as a child between my warring mother and father. No matter what I thought, expressing it would only make one of them unhappy.

"Just tell me what happened," I said. She filled in the details, which seemed to help calm her.

The boy was an athlete and a musician. If he lived, which was still an open question, his future looked bleak. As she talked, it became clear that no matter how much of my sermon I still had to write, I was going to have to use some of my few remaining hours of writing time to hop a train to Philadelphia.

At the hospital, I spent an hour and a half with the family, visiting the young man, holding his hand, and talking them all through this incomprehensible disaster. On the way back, my anxiety had subsided. I had experienced one of those rare moments when I heard the call and answered, *I am here, as I am.* A test with one right answer. Of course, I was able to finish my sermon on time.

The young man lived. After his initial rehabilitation, I sent a letter to the congregation about his misfortune, saying, in effect, that as a community we should do whatever we could to make his life as comfortable as possible. A congregant in the auto business had offered to help us acquire a van specially outfitted for a partially paralyzed person in a wheelchair, but even with the insider's price, it would cost $50,000 to outfit it.

Two days later, I walked into the synagogue offices and was greeted with extra cheer by my secretary. "Matt, how are you doing? If you need help opening your mail, just let me know."

"You've known me now for a year and a half," I said, wondering if there was a prank afoot. It wasn't my birthday. It wasn't April Fool's Day. "I always open my own mail."

She attempted to stifle a grin. "You better go take a look first."

On my desk was a huge pile of hand-addressed envelopes. The next morning there was another, bigger pile. And again, on the third day. I opened every one myself, incurring numerous paper cuts all over my hands. By the time all the mail had been opened, we had the $70,000 plus an anonymous check for $25,000 from a single donor to help with related expenses, like hiring drivers.

I knew then that no matter what challenges we would face as we grew and evolved as a community, our core values were solid and in line. It was going to be alright. To this day, whenever I open my mail, I think of those stinging injuries as spiritual reminders of what it means to be a rabbi, to truly answer the call and be present for whatever I may find on the other end of the line.

CHAPTER EIGHT:

Can We Agree on Anything Anymore?

In the midst of this already off-kilter year, 2008, the Obama/ McCain election gave us something more uplifting to focus on. At that time, I would estimate that our members were mainly centrists or slightly left or right of center, politically. There were a lot of people rooting for John McCain, who seemed to be the last of a dying breed—an old school Republican who could maintain a moderate stance and work with people on the other side of the aisle. If he had chosen Joe Lieberman as his running mate, as was briefly rumored, many of the people I know would have leapt at the chance to see a Jewish vice president in our lifetime and voted for McCain. But when he chose Alaska governor Sarah Palin instead, the tide turned swiftly in favor of Obama. Northeasterners just couldn't stomach Palin. She wasn't articulate, she didn't seem qualified to take over the presidency should something happen to McCain, and her place on the ticket seemed purely strategic, an attempt to lock in the burgeoning far right part of the Republican party that many in our part of the country didn't like or understand.

Personally, I couldn't have been more excited about voting for Obama, and the feeling was mutual among many of my friends and colleagues at B'nai Jeshurun. Once McCain was no longer an option for them, even the more right-leaning members in our community threw themselves headlong into the excitement of helping to elect our first African American president. Obama's rallies were filled with an optimism and energy we hadn't known for a long time, and his signature "Yes We Can" campaign slogan seemed to lift us up, especially after such a difficult year. I can remember grandparents in our congregation telling me that they were elated to be a part of this historic moment—it was something they wanted to tell their grandchildren about.

When Obama won, the excitement was like nothing I'd ever experienced. There were tears of joy and dancing in the streets. We pulled all the children out of our nursery school classrooms on inauguration day to let them watch history play out on television. Most of them were too young to appreciate the "show" on TV that day, but that seemed beside the point. There was something existential about this moment. We were thrilled that a new generation would grow up knowing that a black man could become the leader of the free world. It felt like a new day in our country, and we all wanted to be a part of it. We hoped that the experience of watching him take the oath of office would somehow make its way into the subconscious minds of these little children and we could help shape a generation that would grow to be kinder, more inclusive, and eventually appreciative of the historical significance of this moment.

Significantly, not one congregant called me to complain that we were propping up an individual from a specific political party. There seemed to be a singular understanding that this was about breaking through an unimaginable social and political barrier rather than celebrating the Democratic Party. My son Jake was then in nursery school, and I remember holding him in my lap, hugging him tightly as tears streamed down my face. If an African American could be elected president of the United States in my lifetime, anything seemed possible. And the fact that I literally did not hear a peep of objection from anyone—in a congregation that was never bashful to share its opinion with me—told me that this was indeed a transcendent event, at least for one day!

In retrospect, that day seems like the end of an era as much as the start of a new one. Once Obama took office, the polarization that had been starting to bubble for some time, began rolling to a steady boil.

Eventually, things began to stabilize in the country, and our community found ways to recover from the financial crisis. As a synagogue, we had to start planning for the future again, and we were able to raise significant money to make our vision a reality. As the market rebounded, people were willing to invest in us again, knowing we'd been there to support them when things had been hard. We were able to do a major renovation, the first since 1968, and B'nai Jeshurun was now looking as fresh and new as it had begun to feel with all the innovative programming and energy of the last few years.

In early 2010, a dear member suggested that we dedicate our new choir loft to our much-loved cantor emeritus. Cantor Summers had served the synagogue for fifty years, and his health was beginning to decline. The congregation wanted to make sure he knew just how much his service meant to the community. Rather than wait for a posthumous honor, we wanted him to enjoy being celebrated while he was still with us and could participate in the service.

Over a thousand people came to the dedication ceremony, and Cantor Summers was beaming. He was able to sing again for the community, and you could tell how much this meant to him and to everyone involved. It was such a beautiful night, a quintessential B'nai Jeshurun gathering, replete with love and joy and honor. I felt truly blessed to have been a part of it, even though I had never had the privilege of working alongside the cantor myself. The event said everything about how much this community cares for its own.

After the ceremony, the woman who was and is known as the matriarch of the synagogue (she had been the first female president of the congregation decades ago and was the second wife of the former senior rabbi) came up to me with tears in her eyes. "Oh, Matt, dear," she said sadly. "I don't know if they will even know to do this for you one day." She patted me on the shoulder and walked on, and I felt more than a little stunned by her statement. I knew she wasn't implying that I wouldn't be respected or appreciated by the congregation at the end of my tenor, but her foresight seemed spot on. Things were shifting in the world of congregational Judaism and religion generally, and I knew it. This woman had been deeply involved in her synagogue her whole life, and she could tell where things were headed. From her perspective, the new generation was not as dedicated as hers (and the ones before her) had been. She was saddened by the thought that we would lose this sense of reverence and community in the future.

That night began with a feeling of euphoria. We had survived our first major crisis as a community together and emerged stronger. We had discovered ways to honor our roots, and founding members of our congregation were still with us to witness our success. It ended with a sense of impending dread. Indeed, studies were coming out around that time showing that synagogue membership in America was lower than it had been for many years, and fewer young Jews were comfortable affiliating themselves with specific denominations. It did feel like we were on a slow road to irrelevance.

This reality weighed on me, of course, as a rabbi who was trying to build up a synagogue just as it was becoming increasingly challenging to find people willing to commit themselves to congregations. It didn't help that things in my personal life were hitting an all-time high for stressors, either. My parents both died within a few years of each other, and our second and third children were born around right before my first parent, my mother died. As I tried to manage the grief over my parents and the sleepless nights with new babies, as well as an existential dread about the future of my career in organized religion, I found myself indulging in poor eating habits again, and before long I had gained about forty-five pounds.

One day I got a call from a woman whose forty-five-year-old husband had died of a sudden heart attack. The husband had been slightly overweight, but he'd been trying to work on it, and in fact, he died while running for exercise. That death really shook me. I was around the same age and in the same position. My kids were babies. I looked at this man's children when I officiated his funeral, and all I could see was how much this family would miss out on—proms, graduations, and weddings would all be celebrated without their father. I felt consumed by fear, and I was determined not to let this happen to me.

The next day, I made an appointment with a cardiologist. What I found out was that if I didn't make major changes to my life soon, I myself wouldn't have long to live. My cholesterol was high, as was my blood pressure. I was officially just heavy enough to qualify as obese. I was pre-diabetic. My mother had died of complications from obesity, and so this diagnosis was just what I needed to wake up and make a plan. I couldn't let myself go on like this when I had so much to live for—Lauren, the kids, and the synagogue were all too important to me. I began another physical and psychological journey to health and managed to lose all the weight I'd gained and develop an awareness about diet, exercise, and nutrition that has helped me not just stay alive, but live a fuller, more confident life.

* * *

While I was healing my body, I also began working on the spiritual crisis I'd been facing ever since the former cantor's dedication. He served the community at a time in history when most people, whether they believed in religion or not—and frankly, whether they wanted to or not—belonged to a church or a synagogue. This was the American way of living. One could even argue that belonging to a local religious institution was a patriotic act back then. During the Cold War, people were constantly reminded that in communist countries, especially the Soviet Union, religion was illegal. Belonging to a church or synagogue in the United States was an expression of our freedom of belief. As Jews who wanted to integrate into American society, regular synagogue attendance was key. Whether or not there was a spiritual experience attached to that attendance was beside the point. People felt obligated to show up for services, and they did so regularly.

In those pre-Internet days, churches and synagogues were meeting places for communities, too, not just places to pray. They were places to gather and socialize on a regular basis. This made it a little easier for clergy to do their jobs. If the pastor, rabbi, or priest asked for something, the parishioners complied for the most part. It just wasn't the American way to defy the cleric.

Of course, times had changed. Like so much else in our lives, religion had become disrupted. Rather than meet up for bingo or bowling or dances at houses of worship, people hung out online, in coffee shops, or at the spin studio. Just as Uber, Netflix, and Airbnb had replaced taxis, video stores, and hotels, now yoga studios, mountaintop retreats, and self-help groups were swiftly replacing organized religion. It was easy to panic and worry that the end was near for professional rabbis like me.

But while the concerns I had about the future of synagogues didn't disappear, I worked to find ways to reframe those worries as possibilities. I became a fellow in an innovative program called Rabbis Without Borders, within a Jewish think tank called CLAL, which allowed me to focus on new and interesting ways to reach people and create programming that worked for a variety of audiences.

At the same time, there was encouraging news about the shifts in affiliation. While the percentage of Americans who belonged to religious institutions had been steadily declining since the late 1990s, a tremendous majority of Jews not only said they still celebrated major holidays like Passover and Yom Kippur, but also that they proudly identified as Jews and believed in God or another type of higher power. I found a real paradox here. From the outside, it seemed like Jews no longer wanted to be Jewish, but as I studied more closely, I realized it was more that they didn't want to affiliate with a synagogue to manifest their connection to Judaism. This was a paradigm bust. The Temple had always been the place where one would demonstrate their attachment to their faith. Affiliation with a synagogue was a huge part of Jewish identity in the past, but that wasn't the case as we moved into the future.

It seemed to me that we were not necessarily becoming less religious as a people, just more hesitant about affiliation. In other words, the interest was still there, but the institutions were not catering to those interests. It was akin to bringing a vegetarian to a steakhouse. She might be starving, but if there is nothing for her to order from the menu, she's going to ask to go to a different restaurant.

Our predicament seemed less bleak than I'd originally feared. We could take the drop in membership nationally as a sign of doom and gloom, or we could take it as an opportunity to revamp how we set a new prospective spiritual menu. This was our chance to add vegetarian options to the steakhouse menu. If we wanted to keep ourselves relevant to young Jews—indeed, Jews of all parts of the demographic spectrum—we were going to have to repackage the synagogue experience we were trying to sell. The content would stay the same, but the delivery would have to change. We had to choose whether to see things as falling apart, or as our biggest opportunity yet.

For the next few years, we forged ahead and looked for new and interesting programs and resources to offer. We did everything we could to revitalize the synagogue experience for the younger generation and reach them where they were at. We created an alternative religious school model—one with less regularity but more intensive time not just with the kids themselves but with their parents as well. Most of these parents had not encountered a rabbi since their Bar or Bat Mitzvahs and weddings. Now, when they came in to spend more time with their children, they were also exposed to a new and relevant brand of Judaism. They became connected to clergy and community in unexpected ways, such as the spirituality apps we developed so that messages of wisdom could reach users on their way to work or while running errands, incorporating Judaism into their everyday lives. We created innovation labs where we tried out new models of thinking and were able to evaluate their success or failure quickly and efficiently.

My vision was to focus on positive psychology as our way into the future of B'nai Jeshurun. Rather than just publishing thank-you notes for generous monetary donations, we'd include notes about acts of kindness and service that our members were doing in our bulletins. We wanted the synagogue to be a place where everyone's relationships were valued and everyone's contributions to the community were appreciated, be they volunteer hours, a new idea, or a dollar donation. Depth of relationship is what religion is ultimately about, and we were intent on deepening that relationship in any way possible.

If people were going to look for yoga classes or self-help lectures anyway, why not offer them here at the synagogue, where they could also connect with other members and build friendships and support networks with us? If parents were going to send their kids to Hebrew school to prepare for their bar and bat mitzvahs, why not make sure that their experience at Hebrew school was not just academic but spiritually relevant to their lives? My staff and I were always looking for ways to combine modern social science and religion to create new traditions, and for the most part, it was working. In this way, the Temple became a center for meaning and improving quality of life. People were searching for something "more" in every aspect of their lives, and we were doing our best to make the synagogue a place where they could come to find that.

* * *

As the years passed, and our membership continued to grow, the country was shifting and becoming increasingly divided. By the end of the Obama administration, the Tea Party conservatives were in full swing, and Americans were fighting over issues like openly carrying guns. President Obama's signature healthcare plan, which was admittedly ambitious and confusing in many of its details, was particularly polarizing. In fact, the very act of taking sides seemed to be the new priority, over and above learning about the issues at hand. This was certainly happening in my own congregation, and when the president signed the Iran

Nuclear Deal, that was the real beginning of the end for any sense of communal unity.

Israel is always a touchy subject for Jewish communities, and the Iran deal made an already fraught conversation absolutely polarizing. Silently, anti-Semitic tropes were beginning to make their way to the forefront of the national conversation. If you were for the deal, you were against the Jews and Israel. If you were against it, like so many Republicans were, you were an ally. In this simplification of a tremendously complex political move, Democrats were attacked as anti-Semites and self-hating Jews, and Republicans adopted a staunchly pro-Israel, anti-Obama position. It was absurd to reduce this complex issue to an either/or scenario, but that was the direction in which our whole country seemed to be headed. It was all or nothing, black or white, good or evil, with no room for any middle ground or even a civil conversation.

Senator Cory Booker, who had come to our synagogue many times and had been hugely popular with my congregants, was vilified when he chose to stand with President Obama on the Iran deal. Suddenly, he became public enemy number one around here, and people were genuinely angry. He was anguished, but there was little opportunity to engage in constructive dialogue. People were quick to lock in their positions, and before long, Israel became a pawn in the political influence game. It seemed obvious to me by now that come the next election cycle in 2016, those same voters who might have chosen McCain had it not been for Palin would be looking for a reason to vote Republican again, and apparently, they'd found one.

It was becoming harder and harder for members of our synagogue to talk about politics without finding themselves in heated conflicts. Tensions were high and, as is human nature, everyone was sure that his or her opinion was correct and that others were decidedly false. This was made more difficult to combat because people on both sides were starting to get their news from social media sources which were programmed to feed them more and more of what they already believed rather than providing them with neutral, unbiased reportage. Division was everyplace I turned. People were not just disagreeing about issues like immigration, guns, and healthcare; they were fighting over them.

To some degree, discord among members of a congregation is normal and expected. But the level of vitriol was unlike anything I had ever experienced, and it seemed to be reflective of trends in the country at large. When one member posted a strongly worded defense of Hillary Clinton on social media, another attacked with counterpoints about Donald Trump. Before long, the post had made its way through our community, and it had blown up into an ugly fight among at least one hundred people. There came a point where we actually felt moved to step in and call a meeting for the people who were actively attacking one another online, to try and calm things down. In normal times, we would never get involved in what congregants post to their personal social media accounts, but this seemed to be beyond the scope of normal times.

As the community grew increasingly divided, I began to think about how we could use the principles of "disruptive innovation" which had been so successful in our social and spiritual programming, to help bridge our growing political and ideological gaps.

Clay Christensen, a professor at the Harvard Business School, coined this useful term. Disruptive Innovation describes a process by which a product starts at the bottom of the market and relentlessly moves up, eventually displacing established competitors. Think of the mainframe computer. It was once a life-changing innovation, but it cost millions of dollars and was enormous. Only large companies could afford them, and the corporations that produced mainframes sank continuing resources into creating more complicated and expensive mainframes, counting on continuing return of their customers. Meanwhile, in garages and dorm rooms, young innovators disrupted the process with the mini, the desktop, the laptop, the tablet and finally the smartphone. Who still uses a mainframe computer?

We, in turn, had used this concept to help reinvent B'nai Jeshurun in my early years as rabbi there, creating more exciting and relevant programming that attracted new members and brought those who had left back into the building. This had been tremendously successful for us, and I knew we needed to keep moving in that direction. But even more importantly, I wanted our synagogue to be a space for people of all backgrounds and ideologies to sit and co-exist together. Every house of worship has a space called a sanctuary—literally, a place of refuge and safety. Sanctuaries have actually provided life-saving protection for people who face danger, and I wanted to be sure that ours would be consistently welcoming and non-judgmental.

What if we extended the idea of our "sanctuary" to mean a refuge where people of different political opinions could come to express themselves and be guaranteed they would be heard, seen, listened to, and not ridiculed for stating their beliefs? Not just a safe space, but what I like to call a *brave space*. A place where people can seek not just a sanctuary but active engagement with their fellows in a spirit of mutual honor and respect. If houses of worship were able to take on the role of honest broker for difficult communal conversations, they could become places where people could express their fears and hopes without the ridicule to which we have become accustomed.

Was it possible for us to agree on overarching religious ethics—for example, that we should feed the hungry—and explore why we as a religious community value that ethic? Would that in turn make us better able to hear each other talk about what makes us fearful, reticent, and even passionate when it comes to manifesting those goals in the world? At the very least, I thought, this approach would help us understand one another better, while simultaneously our religious institutions could become much-needed centers for community connection, increasing their relevance and helping them thrive once again.

After all, Judaism teaches us that we should treat one another as we would want to be treated ourselves, for we are all made in the image of God. If we are all valuable representatives of God, we should be able to find ways to argue our different points of view peacefully and with mutual respect.

Of course, when we engage in these difficult conversations, we must recognize that there are boundaries. We cannot sanction outright hatred and bigotry. But we do need to make room for people to express the natural fears that comprise our particular biases. In this way, our sanctuary has to be a space for authentic sharing, even if we say things that put others off. We all have fears that manifest themselves in different ways. If we understood that each of us carries our own demons and unique internal battles based on who we are and where we come from, we might listen a little more intently and understand what others are saying.

If I, as a rabbi, could commit to putting aside my own political commitments in the name of communal progress and evolution, perhaps others would follow. I wasn't looking to foment a revolution, but instead to nurture the evolution of our community into one that could genuinely consider multiple conflicting viewpoints with respect. This would be the focus of my rabbinic practice for the foreseeable future.

CHAPTER NINE:

Pulling at the Strings of Our Souls

We were already a feverishly polarized nation before the 2016 election cycle, but we had no idea what was to hit us afterwards. Every reputable poll published right up to election day indicated that Donald Trump would lose to Hillary Clinton by significant numbers. Almost no one thought he had a shot at becoming president. None of his supporters who I knew thought he would win either. Liberals viewed Trump as a joke and never believed he would be taken seriously. The "election ticker" that *The New York Times* published daily never had Trump at higher than a 35 percent chance to win. And yet, candidate Trump's rallies were packed with an almost cult-like following that, in their own way, had the same level of zest and energy that candidate Obama had at his events.

When he won the election, at least half the country was in utter shock. Some literally couldn't believe that such a person had been duly elected to the highest office in the land. Who *were* these people who had come out to vote for him? Why *did* we still operate with the electoral college system when the popular vote was unquestionably in favor of Hillary Clinton? Even Republicans seemed surprised at his unexpected win. Trump himself looked a little stunned when he came out to give his acceptance speech.

The morning after the election, like so many other parents, Lauren and I struggled to explain to our children, who were now fourteen, eleven, and nine, what had happened. We wanted to assure them that while the results of this very unusual election were not what we had hoped and assumed they would be, we still believed deeply in the strength of our democracy and in the system of checks and balances that would help to keep things calm for the next four years. We would still be able to fight for the things we believed in and continue to work against injustice, civil intransigence, hatred, bigotry, sexism, and xenophobia. Presidents come and go, we told them. But the citizens of this great country are the ones who ensure our values are lived day to day. There was a great sense of purpose bubbling beneath the surface, a tremendous drive to engage in peaceful protest, to write to our representatives about the causes we held dear, and to help elect leaders in midterm elections who might offset the Trump agenda. In fairness, we didn't know exactly what Trump's political agenda would be like, but we were horrified by the way he acted as a human being.

It was clear from the very start that this presidency would be tumultuous, and it was therefore more important than ever to help my family and my congregation remember that how we react and operate on a daily basis would be our most effective path forward. As someone who was raised to respect the office of the president, I would do my best to give Trump the benefit of the doubt. I encouraged my congregants to do the same, in hopes of helping to set a calmer and more rational tone.

I made it clear to my congregation that I had not voted for Trump and that his election was disappointing for me personally, but that I disagreed with the idea of blocking legislation blindly without first considering its merits. I hoped our synagogue would be able to withstand the tensions between members who disagreed on politics and come together to fight for things we all believed in. Any person who acted with love and compassion and kindness would be welcome in our community. We were all children of God, and we all deserved that respect and inclusion.

In those early days, I did everything I could to be non-partisan in my approach. I wanted to fill the confusing space with a call for connection, empathy, and understanding, and the feedback I got from my congregation was mostly positive. People were grateful that I acknowledged the shock of this new day, and they were thankful for my call of unity. Nonetheless, the disconnect between the two sides was the worst I had ever experienced, and I knew that the next few years would be challenging for us all.

Around inauguration day, I wrote a prayer for the new president and gave it as my sermon. We also posted it on social media, hoping that by expressing compassion I might inspire others to do the same. I prayed that the new president would be successful and stem the tide of our complex national problems. I vowed to use my democratic right to protest when I disagreed with his policies and to advocate when I agreed with them, not for the sake of political partisanship but for the sake of good and decent ethics and values. I prayed for his health—both physical and mental—and for the safety and well-being of his family. And I prayed that he would not let himself be diverted by the chaos of politics but instead focus on how his words would now move markets, open or close businesses, and start or stop wars. His language now had the power to encourage people to understand or dismiss each other, to believe in hope or cultivate our darkest impulses. His finest accomplishment could be melding together the disaffected world into which he had tapped with other parts of the nation who were searching for a better tomorrow.

This wasn't lip service on my part. I really believed that the power of the office might help guide the new president to see the opportunity in front of him. Perhaps his propensity for breaking norms would help him reach both sides and leave the fringes to themselves.

Finally, I expressed my hope that Trump would be granted a depth of spirit which would afford him thick skin, allowing him to find generosity when he encountered the slings and arrows of his opponents:

> *A big spirit, after all, makes for a small ego. A small and healthy ego makes for a generous heart. A generous heart makes for a brave soul. A brave soul makes for openness of community. An open community makes for crea.5tive productivity. A productive nation will make for prosperity. Prosperity and love will make for a grateful nation. A grateful nation will make for a fulfilled president.*

In this prayer, I expressed the hope that I could eventually trust and perhaps even respect this person who was now our country's leader.

Of course, as soon as that prayer was published, I heard about it from every possible perspective. From the left, I was excoriated for simply acknowledging Mr. Trump as the president. I was accused on social media of supporting misogyny, sexism, and racism because I had extended Trump my best wishes and hopes for the future. From the right, I was accused of being pedantically apologetic. "What's the matter?" one commenter asked, "You think he is so ill-equipped that he needs your prayers?"

The letters and phone calls were coming in constantly. On the one hand, you always know you are doing something right when you get attacked from both sides—this means that you are firmly planted in what some political thinkers have called the radical middle, that dynamic place where you can reach and relate to both sides of a conflict. On the other, it felt like I was stuck in quicksand, and every time I reached out to one side or the other, I would sink down even further.

I had been looking for a way past the vitriol, to a place where people might realize that my true goal was to engender healthy dialogue. I didn't hide for whom I had voted, but I made it clear that I absolutely accepted Trump as the president nonetheless. I wanted my children and my congregation to see me as an exemplar of generosity who could open my heart, even when I felt pessimistic.

But hearts were already hard, and in those first frenetic weeks of January 2017, the proverbial fire hose just kept on coming at us. Part of it was the fear so many felt, and part of it was a White House that seemed to be out to make its point and keep its promises without subtlety or nuance.

The major crescendo came a few weeks later when President Trump instituted his initial travel ban. As I mentioned earlier, my family went to the airport to demonstrate because we felt the president's actions against Muslim immigrants were the antithesis of Jewish values. My wife and I wanted to model positive social action for our children, and I wanted our family to do the same for my congregation. Knowing that my action would evoke passionate responses from all sides, I wrote yet another public letter, urging my congregants to pay attention to how the issue of immigration might begin to cross our lines of ethics and to act in accordance with our tradition to advocate for change when necessary. In "normal" times, I would write only four or five of these open letters to my congregation each year. To write three like this in about six weeks said a lot about the days we were experiencing.

Once again, I found myself opening hundreds of emails and fielding dozens of calls every day, many of them from incredibly angry congregants. There were vicious attacks on social media and some from within our own community. That week I received one of the most insulting letters of my career, stating that I was a rabbi who only cared about money, who brainwashed children, and didn't care about those who vote on the right, signed: "The Congregation B'nai Jeshurun Millburn/Livingston Trump supporters."

Some of these families left our synagogue that week; others would follow soon after. Still others, though, were relieved to know that their rabbi was willing to stand up and take action in the name of Jewish values, and hoped that I would continue to do so, even if that meant I had to cross over the political line

I usually tried to avoid. What I experienced that week was a microcosm of what was unfolding in the country at large. It was a chance for us to prove we could break from the national path of ultimate polarization, and I remained hopeful that we could find a way to move forward together.

In one of the many conversations I had that week, I made the analogy of how we view an umpire at a baseball game. I recalled coaching my kids' baseball teams and feeling baffled by an umpire's seeming disregard for the pleas of our team when the play was close. When my son started to work as a teenage umpire, I saw coaches and other parents acting the same way I had, but this time, towards my son. I couldn't believe adults would treat *my* son in such an egregious manner! Our perspective changes when the shoe is on the other foot. Yet we aren't always lucky enough to switch places like that if we see life only through our own point of view. That means we really have to listen to what others are trying to express. In all those phone calls and emails, I did my best to truly listen. Listening would continue to be one of the hardest parts of my job for the next four years, but it was also the most rewarding.

* * *

At the start of 2017, Americans quickly retreated into our own safe spaces to find comfort and companionship. Republicans rejoiced in victory as even those who had publicly declared Trump unfit for office during the campaign now looked forward to getting their agendas front and center after eight years of a Democrat in office. Democrats recoiled in disgust, determined to pull together as never before to fight for the causes that were now in danger and to protect the legacy of Barack Obama. Before long, the country as a whole had braced for a social civil war. From day one, we began to see tribalism rear its ugly head.

In my own community, many people shared my concerns, but there were also plenty of people who had voted for Trump. Most compelling to me were the people who had flip-flopped from Bill Clinton in the 1990s, to George W. Bush in the 2000s, followed by Barack Obama and then Donald Trump. When I saw the switching of sides, I started to understand something not just political, but spiritual about our country. People were searching for answers to society's most significant quandaries. I started to sense from conversations that some people were losing faith in the system of government itself. They saw what they perceived as wasted tax dollars and so they searched for the candidate who would make the actual system better. By now, they were ready for a candidate who promised to simply blow up the whole system.

I serve a synagogue whose population has what it needs on the surface, but many, despite their superficial comfort, started to roil as it related to the government's ability and competence to lead. At the same time, although they were from the exact opposite culture, people in the Rust Belt seemed, for different reasons, to be going through the same thing. They were promised over and over again by each party that their lives would be made better, but each side had disappointed them. It seemed that Trump tapped into a communal disappointment, or perhaps even rage, and that was in large part what got him elected.

As a spiritual leader, I try to express the importance of being aware of other human beings, of their thoughts, feelings, and worries. It isn't realistic for us to stop and look into the eyes of everyone we pass on the street, but we can acknowledge the people around us as equals whose existence has equal importance. If our own lives matter, so do the lives of everyone else who walks this earth. We all want to be seen, heard, and acknowledged. Yet too many of us disparage others, dismissing them as repugnant and alien. No matter how many walls we build—literally and figuratively—we will always live in close proximity to those who are different from ourselves.

One of the most important manifestations of spirituality for individuals is the ability to be aware and present in our existence. But in the broadest sense of the word, spirituality involves understanding what is most deep, beautiful, and authentic about the world. It means we don't forget the miracle of being able to breathe, see, walk, feel, wonder, watch, and worry. It means we understand the miraculous nature of the rising of the sun, the waves' continuing locomotion, the awesome majesty of the glacier, the mountaintop, the desert. All of what exists around us is actually extraordinary. We have to remember to stop, be aware, and be thankful.

Now, we were quickly losing our grasp of this greater perspective. Our spirituality was being overtaken by short-term political passions. Everyone was anxious and upset—and for good reason. After the economic catastrophes of 2008 and 2009, we were all watching our financial tails, worrying that we might easily head into another Great Recession. Almost twenty years after 9/11, and after witnessing regular attacks in Western Europe, we worried about terror. A multitude of concerns riddled our hearts: our children's safety in school, rampant drug addiction, teenage anxiety, depression, and alarmingly increasing suicide rates—all of it was taking a toll on the American spirit. And then this election happened, and we reached a sort of universal tipping point.

Most of us saw these problems as our own, not as the collective plight of others suffering alongside us. We walked past people, stuck in our own cycles of worry and despair, not considering that they may have been feeling the same way. Our capacity for generosity, for opening our eyes to the travails and needs of others, diminished a little more with every passing day. This pattern concerned me not only as an American who wanted to see my country unify, but because of what it implied about the future of humanity at large.

In the months between the election and Trump's inauguration, I heard story after story of families at odds. Siblings stopped talking to each other because they couldn't get over the fact that their own flesh and blood voted for one candidate over the other. Believe it or not, I saw a few couples go through divorces that they blamed on the election. These marriages most likely had significant problems before the election, but when pressed, they would say that they were absolutely filing for divorce because they couldn't live with their partner's politics. Thanksgiving was a time of deep division for families who had members of both parties trying (often unsuccessfully) to sit together at the able. After years of being able to "agree to disagree," they found themselves unable to get through a meal without fighting.

With every passing day, divisions in the country grew deeper and were more visible due to the prevalence of social media, cell phones, and news outlets that were obviously biased towards one perspective or another, rather than being neutral and factual.

Those who lived on the coasts looked down on those who lived in the middle of the country, characterizing them as out of touch, undereducated yokels. Middle America considered those of us on the coasts to be latte-drinking elitists who didn't understand how this country truly worked. We say we live in one country, but we often talk about our fellow citizens like they come from a different planet altogether. I hear it all the time. People deride others from different geographical locations as just not "getting it" and not being enlightened to the "real truth."

I've heard many Jewish people over the years express concern about their safety when visiting rural parts of the country. Historically, Jewish communities are clustered in urban areas— big cities with liberal governments. Just like American travelers in Europe pretend to be Canadian to avoid conflict, Jews traveling in majority white, Christian areas of the South and Midwest will tuck in their star of David necklace or hide their yarmulke under an unassuming baseball cap, "just in case." There is often a distinct unease, an intrinsic worry about anti-Semitism when we travel outside of our safe spaces in the bigger cities. Whether or not the threat we perceive is justified, the fact remains that when one feels out of place, one feels in danger.

Years ago, when I had just finished rabbinical school, I went on a road trip with one of my classmates through Texas. There were incredible rainstorms that week, and we spent much of our time trying not to hydroplane into the side of the road. Once, when a storm finally cleared, we happily turned up the Rolling Stones and set our cruise control to the maximum speed limit of seventy-five, trying to make up for lost time. Within minutes, we saw the telltale sight of flashing lights behind us. We pulled over and the officer parked behind us. He walked up to our window and angrily told us to get out of the car and stand by the side of the road. Although we hadn't broken the speed limit, we seemed to be in big trouble.

For some reason, the police officer asked us what we did for a living. "I'm a rabbi," I said. I had only been ordained for a few days, but I was a rabbi nonetheless. The officer looked irritated. "You're some kind of preacher, boy?" he spat. I nodded, "Something like that, yes." He asked if I was Jewish, and I said yes. In that moment, I began to worry. The interaction was so bizarre. Here we were in a different state, being pulled over for an unknown traffic violation, and now questioned about our profession and religious affiliation. How was this relevant? A moment later, the officer told us to get back in our car and get out of town as soon as possible. I never did find out why we had been pulled over. But I will never forget that instant of fear when I wondered if I needed to keep one eye open for men in white hoods. Whether it was merely my own bigoted projection or the reality of the situation, this interaction reminded me that there are still parts of our country where Jews are not welcome.

Beyond the fear of anti-Semitism and racism, being in new environments can be just plain unsettling for anyone, of any faith. As we began to ask questions like, "Who *are* these people who voted for Trump?" we also began to notice how foreign we all seemed to each other. I remember going with my family on vacation to Utah, where we saw people openly carrying firearms, wearing cowboy hats, and enjoying a night out at the rodeo. It was all fantastically foreign to me, like something out of a Western movie. I had never been to a rodeo and wanted to go, but only my middle child, Talia, was interested in coming along. We both felt like fish out of water—the way people spoke, their syntax and accents, made me feel like I was in a different country. I was as uncomfortable there as I had been when I took my son to a soccer game in London years earlier, unable to understand the lingo or predict what would happen next. Suddenly, those of us who had lived comfortably in our trendy coffee shops found ourselves at a rodeo with the rest of the country, seeing the parts of the United States we had ignored for so long bubble up to the surface and make themselves known. So many of us—frankly, on both sides of the political spectrum—were feeling unseen or unheard at a time when we were all looking for the same sense of safety and security. As the ground shifted beneath us, we would all have to think deeply about our personal connection to political topics. For me, much of this deep thinking was grounded in religion and spirituality and how I would be able to serve a synagogue community that was facing its own divisions and tensions.

* * *

Sadly, one of the biggest outcomes of the Trump presidency was an uptick in the expression of racism and anti-Semitism in America. His now infamous statement about there being "very fine people on both sides" of a horrific conflict in Charlottesville, Virginia, in which white supremacists marched along chanting, "Jews will not replace us" at a "Unite the Right" rally, had one of the most significant impacts on this trend. The media did take this sound bite out of context: Trump quickly clarified that the "very fine people" to whom he referred were those who came to protest for and against the removal of a statue of Robert E. Lee, and not the extremists who ultimately perpetrated violence. Yet the damage was done as soon as the words left his mouth.

It was certainly a tense time to be a Jew, but even in 2017 I felt we would get through this "blip" and things would go back to what we had always considered normal. There would always be a low-level buzzing of anti-Semitism, but I thought it would soon quiet down and we would be able to live in peaceful co-existence with the majority of cultures in America. Below the surface, however, in online chat rooms and on extremist social media platforms, hate groups were increasingly posting anti-Semitic conspiracy theories and gaining a growing audience of Americans. Not only were far-right groups espousing hateful rhetoric, but the anti-Israel sentiment on the far-left often veered into blatant anti-Semitism. Many of us were unaffected by this slow and steady rise in online hate groups, until something truly horrific happened in Pittsburgh less than a year after Charlottesville.

It was a rare Saturday morning when I was not at my own synagogue. My family and I were actually celebrating Shabbat at Rodeph Sholom in the city, where my niece was having her bat mitzvah, and I was joyfully helping to officiate there. Because my whole immediate family was with me, I was happy to turn off my phone and focus on the joy of the day. I was with my beloved former congregation and enjoying the moment of being able to be both rabbi and uncle for my niece on her big day. It was a beautiful service, and I was overjoyed to be there. As the service ended, and we gathered our coats and bags and began to make our way to the party, I turned my phone on to check for messages.

There were not just a few messages, but hundreds. The phone was buzzing like crazy with alerts and emails. Jumping from one text to the next, I began to piece together what had happened. A man had walked into the Tree of Life synagogue in Squirrel Hill, a Jewish suburb of Pittsburgh much like Short Hills, New Jersey, in the midst of a Shabbat morning service. He pulled out a gun and began shooting. We would find out later that eleven congregants were killed that day, and six more were wounded.

I did my best to stay present at the family celebration while keeping myself tuned in to the news as the terrible details emerged. My colleagues in Pittsburgh were on lockdown, and my assistant rabbis in New Jersey were already gathered together to begin responding to the tragedy, writing a letter to the congregation, forming a plan with other faith leaders for a solidarity vigil, and with our educators about how we would explain this to our students. As I danced with my family and tried to compartmentalize, I was getting calls left and right.

By the time we drove home that night, the details of the attack had been released, and I was in full swing, trying not to let the shock of the crisis overwhelm me so that I could do my best to respond to it. The gunman had posted on social media that he was angry with HIAS, the Hebrew International Aid Society, for supporting refugees. When he was finally arrested, the shooter told police that he wanted all Jews to die.

The next day, as the nation reacted to this unspeakable tragedy, we organized an emergency service at B'nai Jeshurun. We had eleven mourner's candles set up in the lobby, each labeled with the victims' names. Over a thousand people came to show their support and solidarity, and the governor of New Jersey addressed the community at a joint, cross-denominational gathering. That week was painful and emotionally draining. I was asked to appear on television for some of the national news shows on which I'd previously been interviewed, to represent the Jewish community in this trying time. At home, we were preparing for the following Friday night, which was expected to be a huge turnout as synagogues across the country urged people of all faiths to attend Shabbat services in support of Pittsburgh and the Jewish community in general. We were also frantically increasing our security measures, installing new cameras, hiring additional armed guards, doing anything we could to make our congregation feel safe.

After a few days, I was absolutely worn thin. We were expecting over a thousand people on Friday, and I needed some time to gather my many thoughts and write a sermon and to just sit with the emotions I was feeling. I remember asking my assistant to please hold all my calls for two hours so that I might be able to catch my breath and get some ideas into writing. Ten minutes later, she knocked on the door and told me I had an important call. It was the Archbishop Cardinal Joseph Tobin, calling to offer his support and extend his condolences to me and to the greater Jewish community. It was one of the most beautiful things to happen in a time of great sorrow, knowing that faith leaders from other religions were holding us in their prayers during this perilous moment.

That Shabbat, I spoke about the importance of giving ourselves the emotional space for mourning. Even though we may not have been personally connected to the victims, we saw ourselves in them—residents of a predominantly Jewish suburb outside a major city. I also urged people to think about why and how anti-Semitism was emerging again and how we could advocate for change and safety moving forward. So much of modern American Judaism has been about being on the defense—reacting when things happen to us. Now was the time to play offense, to be loud and proud, to embrace our identity and show the haters that we will not be made to cower in fear when we come to services, or celebrate our holidays, or support Jewish businesses.

This is a message in which I deeply believe, but I recognize that for many people, events like the Tree of Life shooting make them want to retreat further and hide their Judaism for fear of being targeted. Certainly, some of my congregants felt this way, and it would take some time for them to feel ready to come back to services and feel safe. Others reported that they were determined to learn how to shoot a gun and were preparing to buy weapons for their homes. A few even asked me about the possibility of carrying a concealed weapon to the synagogue for services, in case they needed to help defend us against an attacker.

Although I wasn't ready for such radical shifts in our practice, when another synagogue was attacked in Poway, California, six months later, those ideas seemed a little less radical. For many months, I would look out at my congregation from the pulpit and imagine our plan of action if someone managed to get past our security guards one day. What would I do? Which was the best exit strategy? Which seats were most vulnerable?

One day, a few months after the attack, I was driving past another synagogue that was undergoing major construction. Suddenly I heard a loud boom, and I immediately panicked, thinking it was absolutely an exploding bomb. In fact, it was simply the crash of some steel beams being dropped a few seconds too soon, a blunder by the construction crew. This was when it truly sunk in: We were living in an unmistakably dangerous time in history to be Jewish, and we were on edge, expecting that the worst was just around the corner. We would have to find a way up and out of this trauma-filled space.

CHAPTER TEN:

At the Drop of a Dime: Covid 19
and Social Unrest

Although the waves of racism and anti-Semitism continued to wash over us during those years, the defining event of this period in my rabbinate was the Coronavirus pandemic, which swept the United States starting in February of 2020. The way this public health crisis would change every aspect of life as we knew it, and the way it would affect the jobs of spiritual leaders across the country, was beyond profound.

I'll never forget the surreal Shabbat services I led in March 2020, when COVID-19 restrictions were still new and shocking to all of us. One Friday night, we had a couple celebrating their *aufruf*—the Shabbat before their wedding. Instead of a festive gathering of all their friends and family members, as was the plan, there were only ten people in the entire sanctuary. The bride and groom stood before the open Torah ark as I led the pre-marriage blessing, holding hands. Her eyes were brimming with tears but not in the usual way of a bride-to-be, overcome with happiness. Already it was clear that nothing about their wedding the following week would be as this couple had planned, and they were devastated.

This was unlike any Shabbat I had ever witnessed. For starters, the cavernous sanctuary of our mid-century modern synagogue, which can accommodate three thousand on High Holy Days, was empty and still. On a typical Friday night, we would welcome about three hundred congregants. On this Shabbat we had to tell everyone to stay home. The piano lid was closed, and the music stands were empty.

A plague was coming, and everything was unfamiliar and uncomfortable. Just days earlier, New Jersey had declared a state of emergency. Grumbling college students were packing up their dorm rooms and moving back home to wait it out with their parents. Businesses sat empty, wondering how they would survive with no customers. A sweeping curfew was about to go into effect that would shut down everything, even houses of worship.

Every day that month, the news had been more unnerving than the day before. Two million people could die in the US alone. Italian hospitals were surrounded by refrigerated trucks full of bodies. The lists of pre-existing health issues that could make you more susceptible seemed so broad as to include everyone, and the list of possible symptoms was just as sweeping. All this and no cure or vaccine in sight.

Avoid crowds, we'd been told. Avoid crowds? Just a week earlier I had officiated at a wedding in New York that had been scaled back because of the Covid threat—from three hundred guests to one hundred fifty. Masks were not yet part of our collective experience. People kissed, shook hands, and hugged with abandon, despite the early warning signs of a pandemic.

I remember driving home that night wondering if my headache and runny nose were early indicators of disease. Was I about to bring home a deadly virus to my wife and three children? Could I keep them safe if I changed into fresh clothes in the garage and slathered myself in hand sanitizer before coming inside?

Everything was happening so fast. A week earlier, a private Jewish high school in nearby Paramus had suspended classes after dozens of its students were potentially exposed to the coronavirus at a bat mitzvah. Two days later, the state reported its first coronavirus death. Then the governor ordered all schools and indoor businesses to close. We were bombarded by new terms like "social distancing," and people were wearing plastic gloves to go to the grocery stores and stock up for what seemed to be the end of days; canned goods and toilet paper and sanitizing products were almost instantly wiped out of stock, and there were limits on how many gallons of milk or cartons of eggs you could purchase in one transaction.

By this Shabbat on March 20, I was catastrophizing. Were we all doomed? Was it just warm in here, or did I already have a fever coming on? The ten of us who came to synagogue that night—coincidentally, both the maximum number of people allowed to gather indoors and a *minyan*, the minimum number needed to hold a service in Jewish law—were there for very different reasons. The young couple and their parents were there for their *aufruf*, a traditional calling to the Torah for a blessing given the Shabbat before a wedding. The family in the back rows were in mourning for a recently deceased relative. Both families were devastated, missing the hundreds of people who would normally be alongside them in their celebration and in their time of mourning. The wedding would have to be suddenly cancelled at the last moment, and the week of shiva cut short for the mourners. It was unprecedented and unsettling for all of us.

In nearly twenty-five years as a pulpit rabbi, I'd never performed a Shabbat service to such an empty synagogue. My voice seemed to boom a bit louder than usual as I chanted the traditional Hebrew blessing over the Shabbat candles: *"Baruch Atah Adonai, Eloheinu Melech haolam, asher kid'shanu b'mitzvotav v'zivanu l'hadlik ner shel Shabbat.* Blessed are You, Eternal our God, Sovereign of the universe, who hallows us with Your commandments and commands us to kindle the lights of Shabbat."

The experience was surreal but keenly spiritual. Sharing that huge, empty, beautiful space were two families at starkly different points in the cycle of life—a marriage and a death—each contemplating a profound sorrow. The mourners had just lost a beloved elderly relative. The bride and groom were grieving for the traditional wedding they'd been planning for a year, now lost in the vortex of a pandemic lockdown. Their wedding was not going to be anything like they imagined.

The bride dabbed at her tears with a tissue. The groom stroked her hand and regarded her with a tender smile as I reminded the couple how anxious they had been about the groom's father. He'd had serious medical problems, so serious that after three separate hospitalizations, he nearly died. It was a high priority for the groom that his father be there to see them get married. Remarkably, he had defied the odds. It was a miracle, I reminded them, that he was even there to witness the *aufruf.* They had a reason to feel grateful.

If ever there was a moment made for a rabbi, a priest, a minister, an imam—any spiritual leader—this was it. There may have only been ten of us in person, but our synagogue had already been investing in the technology to live-stream our services before we knew how necessary that technology would soon become. We had multiple cameras in the sanctuary, including one inside the ark facing out so people could see my face and those of the cantors when we turned toward the Torah. For years, we had been streaming Shabbat services and the High Holy Day services for travelers and the homebound, and this week was no different in that one respect. Luckily, we were ready with a spiritual lifeline for a congregation of more than one thousand two hundred freaked-out families (over five thousand individuals) doing what people do when they're freaking out—going back to their spirituality, to their gods, their communities, their roots. I wondered how many would actually tune in on this Shabbat, especially those who were also planning a wedding, or anticipating a death in the family, or who had youngsters attending our early education classes, or teens in our after-school program.

Every weekend during the school year we perform an average of three bar and bat mitzvahs, often followed by a large party. Hundreds of families were likely already wondering if this virus was going to sideline their events. For the momentum of a busy synagogue like ours to suddenly grind to a halt was jarring and worrisome for everyone. Already, messages had been pouring in from anxious congregants, some of whom assumed *their* important religious traditions would be exempt from these new rules.

We had to be the bearers of the bad news that we were going to err on the side of caution, over and over again. For maximum safety, we were going to have to shut everything down.

This news was not going over well in a community of people still adjusting to a new and ever-changing reality of life in a global pandemic. Every day, more businesses closed and more restrictions were applied. Children were home from school and parents were trying to work from home. As a prosperous congregation filled with some people who are used to controlling their environment, this was frustrating to say the least. As a rabbi, I knew I would be one of the people who bore the brunt of this frustration.

"How can you ruin a child's big day, one they studied for and sweated over for a year! It's a bar mitzvah, for God's sake! A bunch of healthy teenagers. After all, they're saying the virus only kills old people!"

"Who cancels a wedding for the flu? We've already sent out three hundred invitations! We'll lose our deposits. It's a disaster!"

"Rabbi, I hear they're still throwing big weddings in Lakewood. Why can't we?"

Lakewood is a town in New Jersey where the majority of the population, about seventy thousand out of one hundred thousand people, are ultra-Orthodox Jews who had refused on religious principle to follow the state guidelines or even to wear masks. The same weekend I led that somber *aufruf* in our synagogue, the Lakewood police had to break up two large Orthodox weddings. By the end of that month, five Orthodox rabbis from Lakewood had died of the coronavirus.

With all these phone calls and emails pouring in daily, I hoped that the example of this couple's barebones *aufruf* would help the congregation grasp that this was just the beginning of a profoundly disruptive period for everyone. I was thinking of the larger community as I tried to console those present and prepare those watching online for what was to come.

"Now life seems very dark," I said. "Those who were planning weddings, bar and bat mitzvahs, and baby-namings will feel great disappointment. We will be officiating at funerals without family and friends. Shivas will be virtual rather than in person. It won't be the same.

"But we're Jews," I continued, stiffening my tone a bit. "And what do Jews do during times of crisis? We thank God for what we have, we grieve for our losses, and we keep going."

That, in a nutshell, has been my philosophy since I became a rabbi, and it sums up much of Jewish history. How have we survived thousands of years of oppression, violence, pogroms, the Holocaust, and all the individual acts of malice directed at the Jewish people? We gather ourselves together, pack our bags if necessary, and move forward.

And no matter what, no matter where, we observe our ancient rituals, especially the Sabbath, which Rabbi Abraham Joshua Heschel, a Polish-American theologian who narrowly escaped the Holocaust, once described as Judaism's "great cathedral." The Sabbath, he wrote, "is a shrine that neither the Romans nor the Germans were able to burn."

After everyone left the synagogue that Shabbat, I popped into my office to check the stats for the live cast. On an average Friday night, a couple hundred people would have logged on. That night there had been one thousand four hundred viewers—a record. I was stunned.

When I got home and told Lauren what had happened, she immediately said, "You have to come through for your people."

"I know," I said. It was beginning to sink in that I was going to lose—for an unknown amount of time—the human contact that makes being a rabbi so fulfilling. "But how?"

"In ways they never imagined," she answered.

Lauren was always full of innovative ideas, and she helped me form a plan of action to get us through those early weeks of fear and confusion, anxiety, and frustration. She suggested using our live-stream capabilities to provide useful information and maintain contact with our congregants. Many businesses, schools, and social organizations were scrambling to figure out how to use video-conferencing and live-streaming technologies, having never needed them before. It was a steep learning curve for many people. We were fortunate in that we had already begun that process, and many of our congregants were already familiar with the technology.

We quickly put together and promoted a series of online lectures, daily meditations, teachings, and inspirational talks. Each week we would focus on one of five subjects. We weren't just going to teach the Torah—we would provide practical wisdom that intermixed with tradition. The first week we focused on the physical body. I interviewed (on Zoom) two doctors about the symptoms of the coronavirus, the science, how best to avoid it, when to go to the hospital, and so on. That stream alone attracted ten thousand viewers!

The next week I interviewed nutritionists and exercise trainers, and we talked about how to maintain our healthy lifestyles without gyms and in-person support networks. Next, we focused on mental health—therapists and experts on childhood development spoke to worried parents about how to deal with kids who were suddenly home from school and isolated from their friends. An ESPN journalist helped us do a live-stream on sports. We interviewed a group of teenagers on Zoom about how the pandemic was affecting their lives.

The list went on and on, and the classes became hugely popular. We all needed to talk, and people needed something to put on their calendar. Couples shared cancelled-wedding experiences. Our cantor, who was pregnant, led a discussion among a group of other women worried about their pregnancies and the complications of giving birth in a hospital under lockdown. After reports of rising substance abuse rates, we did an episode on addiction. Then a book club focused on books about Israel. We were clocking thousands of participants every week.

In the most counterintuitive way imaginable, we went from seeing our congregants intermittently at Shabbat and the High Holy Days to seeing almost all of our people online every week. So far so good.

But the battle to save our congregation was just beginning. What would happen in the fall if we couldn't hold in-person services for Rosh Hashanah and Yom Kippur? Would our families stick by us and pay their membership fees? Would our community survive the pandemic? Would God still be there when it was finally over?

These were the questions with which rabbis and other spiritual leaders worldwide were grappling. How could we find ways to bring meaningful content and connection to our constituents without physically bringing them into our houses of worship? Things were moving at warp speed in every facet of life, and religion was no exception. Among all the stress and chaos the sudden changes forced upon us, there was also a sense of excitement; for innovation and evolution is stimulating and can often bring about the best in us. Although it was clear we had a long road ahead of us, I was grateful for the technology that allowed us to pivot and adapt and which provided us means of connection in a time of extreme isolation.

* * *

Two months after the lockdown began in New Jersey—on a muggy, overcast day in May of 2020—I showed up to officiate at a burial only to discover to my horror that, for the first time in twenty-three years, I had gone to the wrong cemetery. For hundreds of funerals, I had unfailingly been where I was supposed to be, when I was supposed to be there.

Today, the cemetery was empty. No cars, no people. Just rows of headstones and a groundskeeper driving a riding mower. My heart began to thump. A wave of heat crept up the back of my neck as I clumsily stabbed and swiped with rubber-gloved fingers at the map on my phone. "Oh no," I muttered into my mask. "This can't be!" I imagined the husband, son, and the rest of the mourners standing next to the open grave, fidgeting and muttering to each other as the minutes passed, wondering what had happened to the rabbi.

The pandemic had shredded my routine, pure and simple. For months, my life had been a succession of emergencies, chief among them funeral after funeral as the virus swept through our congregation. Before the lockdown, it was sometimes possible to go a month without a funeral. In the first two and a half months after the lockdown began, we had about forty—four a week. A dozen of those were officially attributed to the coronavirus. Many of the others were people who had been in ill health before the pandemic but whose death was likely hastened by turmoil in the health care system. Deaths typically spike during periods of high stress, and this was certainly one of those times.

As a spiritual first responder, my work is defined by the rhythms of birth, life, and death. When a loved one dies, the rabbi often gets the first phone call. That's in part because the single most sacred act in Judaism is how we bury—if at all possible, within twenty-four hours of death. So, whether someone dies at 2:00 a.m. or on a day when I've taken a long-planned getaway with my family, it's time to pop into action. Jewish tradition dictates that a body should be buried as quickly as possible after death, so there is no time to lose once a loved one is gone. As a rabbi, it is my job to coordinate with the funeral home and the cemetery, as well as to console the family and work with them to draft my eulogy for their loved one. It is sacred and important work to pay respect to the loved one who has passed and to help the family begin their process of mourning.

Only once in twenty-three years had I been late to an official function—a wedding. That was embarrassing, but not so transgressive a blunder as showing up last for the burial of a congregant, especially one I had known, with her husband, for almost a decade. She had lived an active life, came from a large, loving family, had a lot of friends, and was actively involved in the community and the congregation.

Before the lockdown, we'd have expected a few hundred people at the synagogue for this service and about fifty for the burial at the cemetery. Now, I had to deliver the painful news to this and many other families that they could have just ten people for the synagogue service and no more than ten at the cemetery. This was invariably received with disbelief at first, then tears of sorrow, and then frustration.

How can this be, those families asked. How can it be that all the people who loved our mom can't attend a service in the synagogue where she worshipped for so many years? How can my dad have lived a whole life and this is all he gets in the end? How can we be robbed of this singular opportunity to honor a loved one with eulogies, shared memories, and to create the narrative that gives meaning to her life?

On occasion, the grief and frustration boiled over into hostility. In this case, it already had. The customary in-office visit to plan the funeral became a three-way Zoom call instead, with the widower and his fifty-something son. When we were connected, I could see the father's face, but the son's camera was pointing down at his legs.

"Adam," the father said. "Fix your camera so Rabbi Gewirtz can see you."

Adam's voice growled back. "He can see my legs. That's good enough."

The tone startled me, but I knew where he was coming from. He fit the mold for a category of most men in their fifties—men in my own age group—for whom Judaism didn't do it for them growing up in the 1970s. During the intake, I asked him about his mother, let him talk and asked follow-up questions. I talked a bit about my own mother. I wanted him to see that I was real, and I wanted to be able to eulogize his mom in a way that reflected his affection for her. Gradually his demeanor softened and by the end of the conversation, he did adjust his camera, and I was seeing his face instead of his shoes.

When I finally arrived at the correct cemetery that day, I had to pull myself together. After making profuse apologies, I handed each mourner a traditional *kriah* ribbon. A *kriah* ribbon is worn at Jewish funerals and for the week of shiva to symbolize the act of rending one's clothing in grief, an ancient practice first mentioned in Genesis, when Joseph "rent" his garments believing his son Jacob was dead. Today, instead of tearing clothing we pin a small black button with a short length of black ribbon attached, the end of which is torn at an angle. Children mourning a parent pin the ribbon over their hearts. Other mourners wear the ribbon on the right side.

When I handed a *kriah* to the woman's son, instead of pinning it on his jacket he hesitated and then stuffed it into a pocket. He didn't appreciate that I was late and it played right into initial discomfort with me in the first place.

I may have won the early skirmish on that Zoom call, but I had not won the battle.

"Thank you, Rabbi," he said before departing. "You really honored my mom."

The next day, his dad phoned to tell me how moved his son was and how relieved he was that his son had come around.

"I don't know if that means you'll ever get him back in the fold again," he said.

I doubted it, to be honest, but I felt good that I had helped defuse some of his distrust and demonstrated that rabbis are more than what he imagined or remembered from his childhood. In this role, you can't take moments of anger too much to heart. When people lose their cool with me, it's rarely about me. Generally, what's happening when someone lashes out at me is classic transference. And the way I deal with transference is to stand firm in my authentic self and be genuine with the person. Once people realize they are encountering the "real deal," they feel more easily disarmed and will let down their guard. I feel confident that when his father's time comes, Adam will call upon me because he knows it will all come not just from my head but from a deep, sincere place in my heart.

* * *

As the pandemic rolled on, death proliferated. Officiating funerals may be one of a rabbi's most important roles—consoling, comforting, and interpreting the unfathomable—but by now the pace of death was becoming almost unbearable.

Thank God we have other clergy, two incredibly talented assistant rabbis, and three cantors who share the burden with me. Still, those months were a crush by any measure. It's my role to keep it together, to be there for others. But I'm, by nature, an emotional person, and sometimes the circumstances are overwhelming.

One of those moments came in the middle of the pandemic summer. We had a devastating but depressingly familiar death. He was nineteen, healthy, outgoing, and well liked. He struggled with intense anxiety but had channeled his nervous energy into designing and launching a line of casual clothing with designs aimed at other young people coping with mental health issues.

The obituary specified no cause of death, but none was necessary—"died suddenly" was the phrase that told part of the story but never the intensely private truth. His name was Jack Nathan and, by all accounts, his death was an accident. He had been at a party with friends and left home that night in great spirits. Life had been going well for him. He was absolutely intending to return home.

Jack was a kid with ambition and a big heart. He wanted his clothing brand to project hope, so he named the line Happy Jack. The business opened online and took in $1,000 in revenue the first day. With a sense of urgency that seems prescient in retrospect, that same day, he personally delivered the $1,000 to a nonprofit that provides mental health services for children, the Child Mind Institute in New York City.

His parents wanted to see his face one last time, so I went with them to the funeral home. The experience was every bit as devastating as one can imagine. There were anguished cries, shuddering sobs, and a promise his father made as he leaned over his son's body to kiss his forehead. "I swear, I'll never let you be forgotten."

As a father of three teenagers, I was powerless to keep from projecting, from feeling in my bones that unique terror that stalks parents. I knew Jack as a member of one of our families.

B'nai Jeshurun had been part of his life from birth—his naming ceremony and bar mitzvah were at the synagogue, and he came with his parents to High Holy Day services year after year. His passing felt personal.

By that time—July of 2020—we were permitted to allow one hundred mourners into the sanctuary because the covid rate was as low as 2 percent. However, literally thousands wanted to be there to both mourn and support Jack's family. Through my tears, I recited the appropriate passages from the Torah. There was no traditional announcement to make about the shiva, the traditional seven-day period of mourning, because there could be no shiva gatherings under pandemic restrictions.

Jack's family was robbed of the chance to be together in the immediacy of their grief, to hear and tell stories about him, to meet more of his friends, and to begin the process of weaving his life and death into the family narrative. His was such a lonely, doleful departure that it helped inspire us to experiment with virtual shivas, which had some amazing and revelatory results.

When Jack's burial was over, the last elbow had been bumped, and the masks discarded, I drove home in a fog and plunged right into an emotional black hole. For four days, I was a zombie rabbi. I don't know if or how anyone gets over such experiences. The children I've buried (and there haven't been many, thank God) I will never forget—none of them, ever.

This year, as the pandemic touched nearly every aspect of our lives, I was grateful as always to be in a firmly established practice of psychotherapy.

If there is one piece of advice I'd give to any prospective clergyperson (and truly, to a person of any kind), it would be to find a good therapist, and stay the course. I have always encouraged my own team of clergy to pursue therapy for themselves, as well as what's known as "supervision"—a kind of professional therapist who helps a clergyperson with issues specific to their job. In this way, one's personal therapist can help with private and overarching issues, and one's supervisor can help work through the professional and ethical dilemmas with which we grapple on a daily basis.

Not only did my therapist help me sort through my childhood trauma and understand how that affected me in the present day, I also learned that I didn't have to carry the wounds of hundreds of congregants all on my own. Often, being a rabbi can be a profoundly lonely experience. You are surrounded by others, yes, but you are also bound by an agreement of confidentiality, and it can be difficult to counsel others without having your own counsel to fall back on.

When I was new to therapy, and new to the rabbinate, I found I tended to try to separate my social life from my professional life. Could a rabbi be seen having a beer with his buddy on the front stoop? Could a rabbi break down in tears on the pulpit after a crushing loss in the community? The first and perhaps most lasting lesson I took from being in therapy was that I could maintain healthy boundaries while also expressing appropriate vulnerability. People may love it or hate it, but if I am moved to tears, I am going to cry—even in front of hundreds of people. Ultimately, I think this ability to express my humanity deepens my rabbinate and my relationships with my congregants, who know I will always be my authentic self with them. I am grateful to have had someone to call after Jack's burial, to process the loss and the fear

and the profound sadness that washed over me so that I could get
up and be ready for whatever was coming next.

CHAPTER ELEVEN:

What is Truth?

The COVID-19 pandemic and the horrific year that was 2020 in America wrapped up with another epic presidential election season. As a nation, we had been stretched to our very limits, emotionally and politically. After a year of enduring a deadly virus in which hundreds of thousands of citizens lost their lives, and after a summer of protest over police brutality and profound racial inequity that seemed to be the last straw in a never-ending haystack of injustice, Joe Biden and Kamala Harris were running against Donald Trump and Mike Pence. To say that there were strong feelings on both sides would be to make the understatement of the century.

No matter which candidate you supported, the underlying sentiment in late 2020 was that your side was unquestionably correct, and the other side was absolutely abhorrent. There were very few "undecided" voters heading into this election. It seemed that everyone believed his or her own "Truth" was the bottom line. We had lost the ability to talk to one another across the dinner table in our own families over those last four years, and in Washington, politicians no longer seemed able to negotiate without being castigated by their own party members. Biden was campaigning on hope, promising to do his best, with all his many years of experience, to reach across the aisle and help restore America. Indeed, I understood what he meant when he claimed that the very soul of this country seemed in danger. I saw it every day in my own congregation, and I knew that this election would indeed be the most important one of my lifetime.

The divisiveness in America at that time seemed impassable. Democrats (and many former Republicans) were fed up with Donald Trump and ready for change. Trumpians dug in for the long haul, willing to overlook all his missteps to keep him and other Republicans in power. It didn't seem possible for anyone to hear anyone else who held a belief system different from their own, much less consider their point of view as valid or take their arguments seriously. It was a frustrating cycle to watch play out daily, and I began to wonder if there was any way I, as a rabbi, could help my congregants move past this.

My team and I met regularly to discuss our strategies for keeping the community civil and safe through this time. Time and again, we arranged to bring groups together in dialogue, prayer, and activities that helped to bridge the ever-growing gaps between them. As a spiritual observer of my community, it is hard to overstate how palpable the rancor had become among our members. I would regularly receive emails with links to articles from each side's echo chamber, trying to prove how the other side was wrong on every issue. There were all-out social media wars between dueling sides that sometimes spilled into the Temple. I always try to remain uninvolved in such battles, but when they began to surface as screaming matches on the carpool line at school, I sometimes had no choice but to call the "sides" into my study to talk things out. I never addressed the issues themselves, but rather the way they were shaming each other in public. Families who had formerly shared holiday meals and carpool duties and planned playdates for their kids now refused to socialize with one another if their politics didn't align. The kids in particular were suffering from this trend. It truly felt like this was the most consequential election of our lifetime. The only thing everyone could seem to agree on was that the levels of anger and communal resentment had grown out of control, exacerbated by the time spent in isolation during the pandemic, while all of our regular routines were upended. Both sides firmly blamed the other for the position our country was in, and no one seemed able or willing to understand other points of view.

For me personally, while I admit that I had agreed with and supported several Trump policies over the last four years, by this point in 2020, I was done. The way he was conducting himself as president and candidate seemed not just distasteful but objectively dangerous. Many of my congregants who had initially supported Trump were similarly fed up and ready for change.

As congregants came to me to vent their frustrations about the election or about their neighbors who seemed beyond the scope of reason, I reached back to a memory from years earlier to give them hope for the future. That memory was from an interfaith trip to Israel and the Palestinian Territories that I co-led with my close colleagues, an imam and Episcopalian bishop. I had visited the Sea of Galilee many times before, but being there with a group of Christians as they experienced the place where Jesus walked on water moved me to tears. I didn't suddenly start believing that Jesus actually walked on that water of course, but seeing the expression of their belief was one of the most spiritually edifying and fulfilling experiences of my lifetime.

The same occurred for me when the Muslims on our trip saw the Temple Mount in Jerusalem, for them the third holiest place in the world. Even with all the conflict between Jews and Muslims over the Temple Mount in mind, I was able to take great spiritual delight watching my Muslim brothers and sisters fulfill their dreams by praying on that spot. Just because our personal truths conflict doesn't mean we can't take fulfillment from one another.

On that trip, we all learned a lot about tolerance and perspective. Many of the Jewish participants assumed that Palestinians were universally anti-Israel, yet none of them had ever met a Palestinian, much less spoken to one face-to-face. We felt it was important to remedy that, and we were able to find a Palestinian who was willing to meet with us and shake our hands. This man certainly disagreed with our politics, but he wasn't about to murder us, and for what it's worth, that was a meaningful revelation for our group. Instead, the Palestinians and Israelis were able to share their narratives in ways that showed our travelers a human side to each story. These stories had little to do with wanting to kill one another and were more about exhaustion and a yearning for a life of normalcy.

I've thought back to that trip many times over the last few years, as our culture in America grows increasingly fractured and as we become less open to dialogue every day. Just as the tiny country of Israel contains many vastly different (and often conflicting) worlds, the US has become increasingly divided, and one group can't seem to fathom another's truth. Harmony in the United States was beginning to seem as distant a reality as peace in the Middle East.

We clergy have a unique role in this dichotomous society. Of course, we all have our own political opinions and ethical beliefs, but we have the opportunity to play the role of mediator, to get people to really listen to one another. Synagogues, churches, and mosques could be places that model ideal communities where people of differing opinion can live and pray together peacefully, focused on their common religion. At their best, houses of worship are places where people practice not just basic civility but also a true openness to the "others" among us. It can be painful to acknowledge that someone's point of view has value and validity, even as it stands in opposition to our own valuable and valid beliefs. As clergy, we can model this willingness to hold opposing truths in one place, to work on our own tolerance and patience, and quell our instincts toward anger and resentment.

* * *

As the election neared, President Trump continued to talk about what he termed "fake news" unfavorable to him and his administration and declared that the only way he could lose would be if there was cheating involved. With the number of conspiracy theories already gaining traction in the country, these statements fanned the flames of those who chose to believe that his win was inevitable, despite the fact that free and fair elections do not have predetermined outcomes.

This concept of attempting to prime an audience for a predetermined outcome was as fascinating to me as it was disturbing. When we study philosophy and religion, we debate issues of Truth with a capital 'T' versus a lowercase 't,' or fact versus belief. Truth, with a capital 'T,' refers to empirical, scientifically proven, logical fact. Truths with a lowercase t are personal beliefs that may be held strongly but are not necessarily shared by every other person or group.

For example, I believe in God. That is my truth, and, interestingly enough, it is a truth shared by more than 85 percent of the citizens of our country. I cannot prove the existence of God, and simultaneously those who don't believe in a higher power legitimately hold that as their truth as well. Neither is right or wrong. Both truths can be valid, even as they are dichotomous.

The same goes for religion generally. I am a Jew. I believe in the truth Judaism teaches. I believe in the Old Testament as my Bible. I believe, in one form or another, in revelation at Sinai, the Ten Commandments, and the teachings of Jewish law. I believe that Jesus and Muhammad were great and wise humans who taught some of the most important values in human history, but they were not messiahs. Obviously, my Jewish faith does not translate into truth for my Christian, Muslim, Buddhist and atheist brothers and sisters, but I expect that we all respect the legitimacy of our truths without trying to impose our own understandings of the world on one another.

Of course, anyone's small t truth can change over time, as our exposure to the world of ideas helps us evolve in our layered manner of thinking. That is why some people convert from one religion to another, and so, too, can people shift in their political thinking. This understanding implores us, when we are in dialogue with others who have different truths, to listen and learn why they adhere to their truths and not set out to change them. Not only can we appreciate and be moved by how others' truths direct their journeys in life, but that understanding can sometimes prompt us to change our own thinking.

We find ourselves in a time when truth with both a capital 'T' and a small 't' are suddenly up for grabs. Many people seem to have forgotten that none of us owns the truth. For any of us to think our belief in how the world works is the only valid viewpoint is maddening. We come up against different truths all the time. We are surprised to know that others think, eat, connect, and love differently than we do. We walk into someone else's home and are shocked by their different traditions around mealtime, recreation, or education. Our nation is vast and diverse, and any truth that is not physically or emotionally harmful to others should be considered legitimate.

We are reminded about our own aversion to other people's truth when we find ourselves acutely angered by it. A religious teaching instructs that when we get downright angry about someone else's belief, the reason for our rage is a realization deep inside of us that something the other person is saying is true. We may not agree, like, or believe what the other person is saying, but on some level, we recognize that this belief is valid to them, and the very validity of a conflicting belief rattles us. For us to successfully navigate a life with other human beings, we have to be okay with such a polarity of truths. We have a better shot of knowing, caring, and trusting one another if we realize that dichotomy is not our enemy. Coming to terms with dichotomy is a key to wholeness within each of us as individuals and to the collective spirit of our nation.

Living in dichotomy can be uncomfortable, and the cliché goes that to understand someone else's life, we must walk in his or her shoes. To truly understand their perspective, we must do everything in our power to empathize with them. This kind of empathy is challenging to achieve because our desire to have others see our truth as *the truth* is so strong that we don't take seriously the call to legitimize other ways of life.

The closest I ever came to this lofty goal happened a few years ago when I was a Fellow at a think tank called CLAL (the National Jewish Center for Learning and Leadership). We were taught to study another person's philosophy of thinking so deeply that we could teach a substantive class advocating their position to others. Rabbi Hillel, an important sage from Jewish tradition, who lived and taught in second century Jerusalem, proposed that getting to know people who believe a contrasting point of view and studying it deeply enough that we can teach it convincingly gives us an unparalleled understanding of that perspective's legitimacy.

I was asked to study the pro-gun position and teach it to a group of students. Of course, I grew up in a home where guns were associated with war, and we would never have owned weapons. However, I've had several formative experiences with guns that have shaped my own opinions on the issue. The first was in the seventh grade, when I convinced my mother I was sick so that I could skip school with one of my buddies. My mother, sensing I was faking, said I had to look after her friend's young son for the day. I also had to do the family's laundry in the basement. My fellow delinquent came over, ready to maximize our day of playing hooky. Seemingly out of nowhere, he pulled a gun out of his bag, saying he'd found it when he rummaged through the doorman's drawer. I had never seen a gun before, and I didn't believe it was real. It looked like a toy, and I was sure my friend was playing a trick on me.

"Come on," I said, "I'll show you it's fake, give it to me."

I took it and was pointing it at the boy I was babysitting until my friend yelled and pulled it away from me. "Look," he said, "it is real," and he opened it to show me the bullets. Our mouths opened wide, and I realized how close I had come to inadvertently taking this young boy's life. Even now, decades later, writing these words sends chills down my spine. I was stupid, naive, innocent, and I should have known better. But I didn't. The gun wasn't locked up, and we weren't being supervised. The stars were aligned for tragedy, and yet I was lucky enough that it didn't happen. The rest of my life would have changed, not to mention the life of that sweet boy, if my friend had waited one extra second before taking the gun out of my hand.

From then on, I was determined that guns had no place in the homes of private citizens. The risks were just too great. By the time I attended this think tank, school shootings had already become a reoccurring event, and I could see no reason for an ongoing proliferation of guns in this country. I had come to despise the NRA and couldn't see any reason why anyone should be able to own guns at all, but I most certainly abhorred assault rifles.

Despite my solid anti-gun stance, I was determined to succeed at the assignment, and I researched the Internet thoroughly, read articles, and wrote out my points coherently. Still, I had yet to get to the place inside myself where I could honestly internalize the pro-gun truth. I needed to try to understand what would make someone sure that they supported gun rights.

My mind wandered back to a night in Brooklyn when I was a teenager, walking with my father and younger sister, when we were violently mugged. Two men attacked us. One knocked my father to the ground and began to wrestle with him, looking for his wallet, and the other held a knife to my sister's throat, threatening her life if we didn't give them all our money. This was forty years ago, but I can still recall the panic in my sister's face and the paralysis I felt knowing there was nothing I could do to help her. I screamed at my father to give up the wallet, and thankfully he listened before anyone got hurt.

Like many textbook liberals, I've never owned a gun. I'm uneasy around weapons, even if it's just a pistol on the belt of the security guards we hire to protect us from domestic terrorists. Their armed presence is a daily reminder of how randomly vulnerable we have all become. Nevertheless, this is the one experience in my life that allows me to empathize with people who want to own a defensive weapon. On that dusky night, on that gritty Brooklyn sidewalk, if I'd had a gun, I would have used it and felt justified. A rabbi—at least *this* rabbi—isn't a politician, rallying one side against the other. My ear is always alert for what we have in common. In the case of weapons, it's fear. I can relate to fear.

When my turn came, I got up and taught the reasons and philosophy behind owning a gun. I channeled my earlier experiences in order to put myself in a position where I could authentically understand why one would want a gun and why one might have a legitimate use for it. In no way did this exercise change my personal conviction about which side of the gun debate I want to be on, but the experience of trying to internalize a truth I reject was useful as I moved forward in my rabbinate during trying, divisive times. In that moment, I thought back to my early days of debate as a student when I still had so much to learn about how to argue effectively and fairly. After so many years, it seemed I had finally figured it out.

Around the time of the conference, I was asked to appear on the MSNBC program, *Morning Joe*—one of my favorite news shows. They have me on two or three times a year when they want a faith leader's view on a specific issue, and that morning, the issue happened to be guns. Right there on national television, something beautiful happened. Someone at the table said that a person like me, born and raised in Manhattan where the response time to a 911 call is about three minutes, would not understand that when a Kansas farmer hears someone breaking into his home and calls 911, he will wait a half hour for the police to arrive. I told the story of being attacked on the street as a kid, and said I could better understand why others would want a gun to protect themselves because of that experience.

Perhaps, given the opportunity, a farmer from Kansas could sit with a rabbi from Manhattan and have a good faith conversation about gun legislation. This sharing of truths might get us to a place where we can ensure the safety of our children at school, without over-litigating the merits of the Second Amendment. Perhaps that conversation would help us each compromise on some of the truths we hold dear in order to reach a higher, universal Truth, like the hope that our children can one day go to school without fear of being killed in their classrooms. I know this is not as easy as it sounds, and I also know that the reason it pulls at the fabric of our core is that it concerns things we have been brought up to care about the most. Part of why this is so complex is that it makes us question the moral relativity of our respective truths.

A precept in Jewish law says that one can always stray from the law if it feels wrong in the pit of our stomachs. The framers of this precept were wise and knew that laws change over time and that somehow, somewhere, someone would take the letter of the law too far and end up hurting another person in the name of legality or truth. They believed that each of us has enough of a gut feeling, enough conscience, to know when something should be followed and when it should not. Following that gut instinct will oftentimes help us make the correct decision, even and especially when the mob mentality is pushing us towards the opposite.

As a religious leader, I want to point out that claiming we own a monopoly on the truth is not only dangerous, it is the epitome of spiritual arrogance. Americans have so many reasons for walking away from organized religion today. One of the primary reasons for religious disillusionment is that so many faith groups and leaders seem to claim that their truth is "the Truth." That kind of thinking not only undermines the prospects for peaceful coexistence in America, it drives a deeper wedge between us. Religion is supposed to build bridges, not create chasms. Religion has fostered war and division, but it has also helped set people free. Healthy religion respects the sacredness of human life while demanding that we see each other in the image of God. Healthy religion teaches that new beginnings are always possible.

Several years ago, in light of how divisive things were becoming in America, I felt I had to leave the Democratic Party and register as an Independent. Having a solid party affiliation was too controversial for a leader of a spiritual community. In my mind, the Democrats were becoming as problematic as Republicans, taking things to the opposite extreme in a way that made me just as uncomfortable, if for different reasons—the notion of "defunding the police," for example, seemed as radical and dangerous as anything else on the table. Obviously, policing in this country could use significant reform, but to suggest simply abolishing the police risks our safety as a society. Many of us can agree that our democracy needs to evolve and get healthier, but Democrats on the far left seemed to suggest we blow up our entire system to get there.

As the radical left grew more volatile in these years, I felt it was my responsibility to call them out publicly, and of course, I paid a price for those statements as well, as I had many times before. Meanwhile, when Biden won the election and I immediately encouraged my congregants to support him and give him a chance to heal the nation, just as I had done when Trump was elected four years earlier, I experienced a backlash from my Republican congregants. It seemed that no matter what kind of opinion one expressed, one was bound to encounter opposition and denial.

Yet I also now knew that getting heat from both sides in this way was a sign that I was doing something right.

* * *

In the weeks and months after the election, Trump and his allies continued to insist that the results were incorrect, that there had been widespread voter fraud, and that he had, in fact, won re-election.

These distortions of fact lead to one of the darkest days in American history—January 6, 2021—when a mob of angry insurrectionists stormed the capitol in Washington, DC, as Congress was certifying the election results. The images from that day were watched live on television and internet channels by millions of Americans.

Watching the chaos unfold on live television was one of the most jarring and surreal experiences I've had. It seemed impossible that people could truly believe they were acting in a patriotic manner as they smashed windows and pulverized outnumbered Capitol Police officers. How had this messy, incoherent "truth" become "Truth" to so many people?

For me, the aftermath was a "what now" moment of epic proportions. Our country was clearly fractured to such an extent that it seemed beyond repair. Something had to be done to move us forward in a healthy direction. After all my years as a rabbi, all the crises I'd lived through, and all the division I'd experienced seemed to be calling me to action right here, right now.

My task in the foreseeable future, like that of other clergy across a tense and divided America, is to help my community rebuild and establish a new dialogue between neighbors of differing views. I now hope to create, not just a safe space, but a brave space, one where people can express their truth without fear of punishment or ostracism.

Healthy religion chooses hope over cynicism, shades of grey over stark black and white, paradox over myopia, dialectic over singularity, sophistication over simplicity, change over status quo, choice over indoctrination, and vulnerability over insensitivity. Healthy religion allows us to question and doubt. It doesn't offer simple answers but teaches us that life is complicated, and yet our faith and our community can guide us through its trials.

Once we recognize healthy religion as the goal, we have to consider not being so quiet. Separation of church and state is a tradition all Americans hold dear. However, there is a difference between respecting this tradition and keeping our faith completely to ourselves. The most important movements for social change in our history have been fueled by religious conviction. Healthy religion has always called for, and demanded, public justice as an act of faith. Where would we be if Martin Luther King had kept his convictions to himself? The Civil Rights movement succeeded because it was first built as a morally-based struggle, independent of partisan politics. Faith in God has been used to hold the nation to a higher accountability, from Lincoln's call for national forgiveness after the Civil War to Dr. King's *Letter from a Birmingham Jail.*

We all know that politics can be sick and can infect us with its sickness, but who will cure and heal religion, if we don't step up and do it ourselves? Are we going to allow suicide bombers to murder in God's name while we shy away from discussions of religious extremism? Faith and God are deeply personal, but perhaps they also need to be public.

The opportunity before us is to learn and be open to positions we may never have considered before, and by doing so, achieve deeper levels of civility in a time where there is little to be found. Clergy should create an honest container of discourse, even when we believe strongly in our own positions and philosophy. We may think that by giving space to other views, we are betraying our core values both as people and as Jews. But opening the door to positions we abhor can deepen our discourse and help us all evolve. This would be staying true to our tradition of *makhloket* and making the possibility of dialectic as wide as it was in the days of the greatest religious thinkers, cultivating argument not for its own sake, but for the sake of heaven.

An extraordinary insight is taught about how the revelation of God's word (and perhaps, we might say, all the words we hear from others) is heard by each of us according to our own capacity. Can we accept that we don't all hear the same utterances in the same way—not because we are bad or good people but because we hear and internalize them differently? If we did, how much could we improve our world for ourselves and our descendants?

As we move into the next phase of our lives—beginning to pick up the pieces from a devastating global pandemic, adjusting to further changes in our government, acknowledging the many difficult and divisive issues we face—how can we work together to hear the call from perspectives other than our own? This is the work I have been trying to do for twenty-five years, and intend to continue for as long as I can.

CONCLUSION:

A Path to the Radical Center

S o much has changed since I first became a rabbi in 1997, and in fact, since I began writing this book just a few years ago. History sometimes seems to move at breakneck speed, and the last few years have been a whirlwind of epic proportions. As a human being, it can be overwhelming to try and take it all in— politics, social justice, poverty, terrorism, climate change, and a global pandemic to top it all off. As a rabbi, I have had a front row seat to the experiences of my congregants as they navigate their responses to these monumental events.

At times, it has been emotionally and spiritually exhausting to shepherd my community through these crises, and as is the case nationally, the tension between people on opposing philo- sophical and political sides can sometimes feel hopeless. There is so much disconnect today that we sometimes assume it is not even worth trying to speak with people whose politics differ from our own. In truth, we have many legitimate reasons not to trust one another, and some of our grudges seem justified.

We fight with each other about everything and spend our precious energy and time trying to decipher the truth. Meanwhile, people are generally down about the prospects for our future. Our economy is slowly recovering, but we are pessimistic about our recovery as a society. Anxiety rates are through the roof, and people only seem proud of their "version" of America. We have allowed voices from the far sides of the political spectrum to claim the media airwaves and general airtime. We have become isolated from one another—not just physically during these extraordinary pandemic times, but emotionally—and we believe we are more different from our neighbors than we actually are.

We know there are despicable people who do and think horrible things. But at the end of the day, people are just people. We all want to make sure we have food to eat, a roof over our heads, a good school for our kids to attend, and better than decent healthcare. We want to celebrate our cultures and religions and be able to live a long and joyful life. We want to be safe from terror and crime and to know that we can live as long as possible. Some think the way to get to this ideal state is by denying the rights and existence of others, but they are a minority. When people come together, they start to understand each other's plight and realize that as different as we are, we ultimately want the same things.

We live in an enormous country, but it's not geography alone that causes us to be different in terms of culture, race, and religion. We are (famously) a nation of immigrants, with families and communities that hail from all corners of the world, a radical social experiment on a scale unknown in human history. With so many diverse perspectives among us, is it any wonder that we reflect so differently on the same events? In fact, it is extraordinary that our democracy has flourished as much as it has.

Still, although technology and advances in modes of travel have connected us in unprecedented ways, we often remain separate and isolated. Main Street does not know Wall Street. The city does not know the country. That leaves us to presume so much about who people are and how they think. We create narratives about each other without actually getting to know one another and breaking down these stereotypes to discover a playing field where we all might be able to play.

The media talks constantly about our being destined for tribalism, secession, even civil war, but I believe we see ourselves as more than merely belonging to groups that think, act, and look like each other. There is a common core to our society, one that is worth fighting for and striving towards. This segment of society—amounting to a substantial majority—has become exhausted by the vocal and sometimes violent extremes that dominate our discourse and no longer identifies with either the right or the left now that both are so extreme and polarized. The party of those I call "radical centrists" consists of people who are fed up with all the angry shouting but who are too often silent themselves. Our silence stems from a desire not to have our heads taken off in daily discourse combined with a sense that in our current political climate, progress and compromise are not ultimately possible. We are not comfortable on the political fringes. If we saw something more moderately forceful, we might get behind and support it. That is the road I believe most of us would follow if it were presented to us as an option.

To get past our tendency to withdraw into self-imposed silence, we need to invest emotionally, politically, ideologically, and financially in a more robust and self-conscious radical centrism. I'm not suggesting we give up on our ideals, only that we recognize others have beliefs that are equally important and from which we might learn and evolve. The more time we spend with people from this newly coalescing radical center, the more we realize that we have much more in common with them than we do with those from the fringes of the political spectrum.

Signs of an emerging radical center are popping up throughout our nation. Think tanks and policy groups like Patriots and Pragmatists and The One America Movement are devoted to bringing people together and helping our nation progress out of gridlock. Their goal is to forge relationships between people who want to come together once again to pursue justice in our country and to build bridges where there are now only chasms. They call us to focus on our country, not our political party. These organizations and publications are advocating that we focus on the parts of policy we agree on and not just the ones we are against.

People are beginning to realize that if we don't unite in common cause, our country and the American spirit itself may be irrevocably divided and destroyed. The premium on national unity is high, and that might mean that justice will come only if we sit with those with whom we don't agree. Not only must we sit with them, we must try to understand that though different from ours, their truth is still valid and that further, we must be willing to compromise and change, to set aside our anger, and move to mitigate the issues that cause the most fear and division.

I recognize the risks involved. Really spending time with the other side will be uncomfortable, to say the least. These moves towards a radical center are also not being supported by pandering politicians because they don't see any political profit from doing so. That's why the people will be leading the politicians, not the other way around. This is the bold direction we need to take, one that can actually change the game from the deadlock culture that plagues us. I am not talking about building a new political party, but a different manner of talking to and understanding one another. We will have to build this out of our exhaustion and anger and out of a commitment to creating building blocks of civility that will give us a shot at a better future.

A dedication to building a radical center demonstrates that we see ourselves as Americans first and that we care most about seeing our long-lasting country thrive and flourish. We can no longer make decisions based on whether they will make us popular with our friends. We have to transcend the high school mentality of thinking only the way our tribe thinks out of fear of being ostracized. Being known only by our political stripes diminishes our identities as human beings, and seeing others that way lessens theirs. The new radical centrism does not ask us to say we are neither this nor that. It doesn't require us to change our political thinking. It's about maintaining our passions and goals while being bold and brave enough to share them with others and to find a way toward common goals by somewhat different roads.

What does it mean to engage in the radical center? It means not abandoning our ideals but perhaps compromising on some of the policy goals that have defined our lives up to now. It means negotiating with others who also want our country to be a better place but believe in getting there a different way than we do. It means believing that expanding our coalition is as important as pursuing our own individual path. It means accepting those with whom we disagree. It means being willing to fall short in our aspirations because understanding the other is vital to our own sense of wholeness. It means getting off of our moral high horses and being willing to engage in debate longer than we thought we could.

Some people characterize this radical centrism as weak—not zealous enough, insufficiently committed to its principles and goals. But if our value system creates boundaries that keep others out, maybe our values don't achieve what we imagined. A truly radical centrism can lead to the formation of coalitions that will transform the world for the better. What more could we ask for than that?

In my own congregation, I have begun to do this work of finding our place in the radical center. For many years I have presented the synagogue as a place of neutral ground, where people who vote differently or otherwise live divergent lifestyles can find commonality in their religious practice and tradition, their moral and ethical values. And for many years, we had some success in reaching across the political divide to find common ground within our community. In general, I am an optimist, and I believe that good will prevail. But at this moment in our history, things indeed feel bleak. I may start each day with hope and faith, but lately, when I go to bed at night, I am less optimistic.

In an effort to put my ideals into action, I have begun to work with an amazing non-profit organization called Resetting the Table, whose goal is to bring together people from across the political spectrum for facilitated discussions about the most vexing issues dividing America today. As RTT suggests, religious institutions are one of the only places still bringing together people of conflicting political beliefs today. In every other sector of society, we have separated ourselves from one another and become increasingly distant. Churches and synagogues have a unique opportunity to engage in "sacred disagreement," which is something I have always promoted.

As it happens, our first RTT training session with fifty members of the congregation was scheduled for the week following the chaotic events of January 6. The heat was absolutely turned up in our country, and the fear was palpable. Even before then, it was difficult to get people to agree to participate in this program. I used my sermon time to plead from the pulpit for congregants to help us make an ideal into reality. I personally invited people both new and established in the community to come. Still, about 20 percent of the people who were invited declined, saying they felt too vulnerable to talk about current events in front of people who were from "the other side." They had lost enough friends and family members already.

The fifty brave congregants who agreed to meet with the facilitators of RTT and participate in the first workshop may have done so grudgingly, afraid of being rejected for their points of view, but they agreed nonetheless, and the results were amazing. We chose a mix of Republicans, Democrats, and Independents, and put them in a room with trained mediators to talk about immigration, anti-Semitism, and reactions to the Capitol attacks from the week before.

The participants were divided into groups with equal numbers of representatives from each political party, with instructions not to reveal their party affiliations or their voting history. After they spoke a bit about themselves and their families, they were asked to react from a values standpoint about the above issues. They had to listen, reflect, and then react to one another and talk about the heart of the matter, not the policy position they preferred.

It was an extraordinary evening. Not only were there no explosive arguments, but the major complaint we received was from participants who were sure we'd paired them up with people who were "too like-minded." They assumed that because they agreed with the tone and content of one another's answers to big picture questions, we must have mistakenly grouped Republicans with Republicans and Democrats with Democrats. Wasn't the opposite the point of this exercise? When we assured them that each group had been an intentional mixture from both parties, they were stunned. Deep down, when we stripped away party polemic, their hopes and dreams for the future were more similar than different. In fact, they were almost identical.

We repeated this workshop with several more cohorts of congregants and with staff and board members as well, and the results have been consistently stunning. The first cohort was so moved by their experience, in fact, that many of them continue to meet on their own to discuss current events and find common ground. Our hope is to continue working with Resetting the Table until we have reached as many community members as possible and done the sacred work of helping people understand they are not so different after all. When speaking from a place of values, not politics, the game seems to change.

The steps we are taking may seem small in the grand scheme of things, but I firmly believe that the more we build relationships, the better chance we have of renewing a sense of our common humanity. I don't see any more important job these days than using Jewish wisdom and spiritual insight to bring people together. I am convinced that we have entered an insidious cycle that plays more upon our emotions than our minds, and it is up to us to break that cycle by whatever means necessary.

As I reflect on my quarter of a century as a pulpit rabbi, I can firmly say that this task of carving out a "brave space" in the radical center feels like the most consequential work of my career. If the events of 9/11 had happened in 2021 rather than 2001, how different would that experience have been? Would we have been able to come together as a city and nation with unified purpose, in communal mourning? Or would we point fingers, lay blame, and make each other's suffering many times worse? If we are being honest, I think we know the answer to that question, and we also know how upsetting and unsettling it is.

But I believe there is a way forward. As always, there is a path to healing, if only we are open to taking the first step and then following through. That journey begins with an openness to truly hearing what the people around you have to say and to being heard by those same people. Together, we can find our way home.

ACKNOWLEDGMENTS

T wenty-five years later, I can still thank God that I am a rabbi. Indeed, I have been blessed to serve two congregations that have long and storied histories. As an associate rabbi, I was fortunate to serve Congregation Rodeph Sholom of Manhattan. There, I was mentored by the generous and wise Rabbi Robert N. Levine and a congregation full of members who taught and nurtured the first chapter of my rabbinate. Sixteen years ago, Congregation B'nai Jeshurun of Short Hills, New Jersey took a chance on a young senior rabbi and I have been utterly blessed and privileged to serve and call them my family ever since. I am in particular debt to the presidents of our congregation and lay leadership who have never stopped trusting me to dream boldly and deeply. We have evolved together and besides my family, there is no greater honor in my life than to call myself your rabbi.

I am thankful to Alys Yablon Wylen who collaborated with me to produce a coherent, distilled, and important narrative. Thank you for your patience and focus. I am grateful also to Foster Winans who listened and processed hours of conversations to help me find my deepest and truest voice. Without your ability to ask the most searching of questions, I wouldn't have been able to find stories that were buried deep inside my soul.

Thank you, Adam Bellow, my publisher and editor, who was not only patient, but also applauded my evolution of understanding religion, community, and politics. You heard my initial message and believed there were kernels of wisdom that would produce a substantive book.

Jane Dystel has been my book agent for almost twenty years. In that role, she has held me to the highest of standards. She never misses a solitary detail and has made me a better writer and human being. More, Jane was once my congregant and more important, has always been a dear and devoted friend. I adore her and her family and hold her in a deep place in my heart.

Thank you, Mark Gerson, who is not only a dear friend, but always encourages me to think deeply and make sure I never stop pushing the world to do and be the same. Mark read the article I published about the radical middle several years ago and immediately encouraged me to expand the idea into a book.

I thank the following dear colleagues and friends whose love, agitation, encouragement, and wisdom live and breathe on every page of this work. It is unfair to list you all without description but doing such would add too many pages. Thank you to the late Rabbi Harold Saperstein, Rabbi Elkanah Schwartz, Scott Hoffman, Steve Ascher, Matthew Turk, the late Rabbi Eugene Borowitz, Jo Kay, Rabbi Camille Angel, Charles Oransky, Emily Terry, Hannah Kates, Lucy Kates, Henry Kates, Bishop Mark Beckwith, Imam W. Deen Shareef, the late Cynthia Wayne, Michael Berkowitz, the late Rabbi Barry H. Greene, Rabbi Irwin

Kula, Rabbi Brad Hirschfield, Rabbi Rebecca Sirbu, the late Cantor Norman Summers, Madeline Dreifus, Charles Dreifus, Harriet Perlmutter Pilchik, Stacy Feintuch, Eric Polans, Sara Polans, Spencer Polans, Rachel Polans, the late Jack Nathan, David Nathan, Brady Nathan and the leadership of the Institute of Jewish Spirituality.

I am profoundly proud of and thankful to my clergy team and senior staff at Congregation B'nai Jeshurun. I am particularly grateful to Rabbi Karen Perolman, who helped inspire my writing, Cantor Lucy Fishbein, Rabbi Leah Sternberg and my clergy partner for so many years, Cantor Howard Stahl. We spend our days doing the most sacred of work together.

Thank you to my most precious gifts in life, Jake, Talia, and Sadie Gewirtz. I know you have sacrificed parts of your lives to allow me to fulfill my calling. It is not just the hours you have watched me disappear to write the words of this book, but the grace with which you have seamlessly grown up in a rabbinic household. You take it all in stride and I think understand the meaning of sacrifice for the good of community and humanity. Mom and I are so proud of who you are as human beings. We love you with every fiber of our beings. You are always first.

There is no one in this world I am more grateful to than my wife and partner of over twenty years, Lauren Rutkin. Simply said, Lauren is the most loving, giving, understanding, patient person with whom I could have ever dreamed I would be lucky enough to spend my life. She is not only accomplished in her own professional life—a leader in our local community—but someone to whom so many look up for advice and wisdom. I could never have a shot at doing or being anything without her. She is

Rabbi Matthew D. Gewirtz

absolutely the greatest ongoing accomplishment of my life. I love
you with every crevice of my being.

And finally, I thank the Holy One of Blessing Who has granted
me with a life replete with blessing and evolution of spirit.